D0729885

STARCHED CAPS

A NURSE'S MEMOIR

NANCY SWAN WHITE

Copyright © 2018 Nancy Swan White.

All rights reserved. No part of this book may be reproduced, stored, or
transmitted by any means—whether auditory, graphic, mechanical,
or electronic—without written permission of the author, except in the
case of brief excerpts used in critical articles and reviews. Unauthorized
reproduction of any part of this work is illegal and is punishable by law.

ISBN: 978-1-4834-8333-7 (sc)
ISBN: 978-1-4834-8332-0 (e)

Library of Congress Control Number: 2018903710

Because of the dynamic nature of the Internet, any web addresses or links contained in
this book may have changed since publication and may no longer be valid. The views
expressed in this work are solely those of the author and do not necessarily reflect the
views of the publisher, and the publisher hereby disclaims any responsibility for them.

Any people depicted in stock imagery provided by Getty Images are
models, and such images are being used for illustrative purposes only.
Certain stock imagery © Getty Images.

Lulu Publishing Services rev. date: 04/27/2018

All the stories in this book are true. They reflect my present recollections of experiences over time. Names and identifying details have been changed to protect the privacy of the people. All the names of physicians, hospital staff, and patients have been changed. In some of the stories, the name of the hospital has been changed. I have compressed some events, and the dialogue has been recreated. However, I have done my best to tell a truthful story.

To the memory of my sister Joyce,
who inspired me to become a nurse

CONTENTS

FOREWORD

Starched Caps is the riveting and fast-paced chronicle of a young woman as she journeys from high school to her nursing career, beginning as a student nurse at a three-year hospital school of nursing, graduating with honors, accepting her first job as a graduate nurse, passing the dreaded state board, marrying her high school serviceman boyfriend, and relocating from her home state of Ohio.

I met the author more than fifteen years ago when we both worked night shift at the former Behavioral Health Center in Greensboro, North Carolina. Initially, I worked as part-time staff/charge nurse on the adult unit, and she worked as full-time charge nurse on the child/adolescent unit. I had taken the job because the private psychiatric hospital where I had served as director of nursing had closed a few years before I reached full retirement age. Although I felt technically retired, I wanted to continue some employment, but without the pressure of full-time employment.

Before the author and I started working together with some consistency on the same unit at Behavioral Health, I had often overheard other colleagues describe her in terms very similar to or the exact same as those my former colleagues used about me—"good nurse," "caring," "exacting," "detail oriented," "thorough." I decided that I must meet this nurse because she sounded like she shared my values and my understanding about the art and science of nursing.

After we met and worked together for a while, I was excited to discover that Nancy was writing a book about her life experience as a nurse. In further conversations, I learned that our past nursing careers had been very similar and contained many parallels. Much like Nancy, following my honor's graduation from a three-year hospital school of nursing in Columbia, South Carolina, and after a few years of employment at several general hospitals, I decided I did not simply want a *job* as a registered nurse. Rather, I wanted a *career* as a professional registered nurse. Consequently, while continuing to work a full-time job and caring for my husband and our four young children, I entered North Carolina Agricultural and Technical State University in Greensboro, North Carolina, where I earned a bachelor's degree in nursing. A few years later, I returned to the same university and earned the master's in counseling degree. I have served as an instructor at two technical schools for practical nursing, and—before becoming a director of nursing—I worked for seventeen years as supervisor of the adult unit at the Guilford County Mental Health Center, High Point, North Carolina.

Starched Caps is a compelling book about the life and career of a caring, professional, enthusiastic, and dedicated professional registered nurse. It offers a realistic picture of nursing instructors, typical and atypical patients, doctors, other coworkers, and students in both clinical and classroom settings. The author's descriptions of essential patient care equipment used in hospitals of the 1950s and 1960s will evoke vivid memories among medical professionals from those eras and, very likely, will inspire giggles and gasps from the nurses of today. Long gone are the Wangensteen suction machines, the Sippy diets, the Acetest tablets, and the enamel buckets for administering the 3H enemas. Six-bed patient wards / care units seem to have disappeared almost simultaneously with the advent of penicillin (no relationship).

This book also offers glimpses of the cultural and political climate of those years, from the stereotypical attitudes and assumptions related to the deep racial divide that existed in the United States to the almost nonexistent role of male nurses.

The book is a riveting must-read for anyone who has ever loved a nurse or anyone who has ever begun or completed the journey to become a registered professional nurse.

Enjoy the journey,

Margaret Brown Burton, RN

December 2017

THE BIRTH OF A NURSE

September 22, 1943, started out to be just another day. It was a cold fall morning in Ohio and the first day of squirrel season. Esther and George had crawled out of their cozy bed early to get the fire in the woodstove stoked up and the coal in the cooking stove started so Esther could cook up a big pot of oatmeal for breakfast. It wouldn't be long before their children would get up and come to the kitchen to sit by the coal stove and wait for their breakfast as they kept warm. After George hauled in extra buckets of coal and an armload of wood, he sat down at the kitchen table and drank a hot cup of coffee. Once the oatmeal was ready, he ate a big bowl of the hot cereal; drank a second cup of coffee; put on his heavy coat, toboggan, and boots; picked up his rifle; and headed out the door to hunt for squirrels.

Esther sat down to relax and read the newspaper. No sooner had she gotten settled down than she heard Kevin, who was one and a half, crying.

1

She slowly got up from her chair and went to his room to change his diaper and get him ready for the day.

The crying had awakened the other children. One by one, they rolled out of bed. First, nine-and-a-half-year-old Joyce; then Janet, five years old; and finally George Jr., who was seven. Once all four of the children were in the kitchen, Esther handed the baby to Joyce to hold while she made toast, filled bowls with steaming hot oatmeal and brown sugar, and poured four glasses of milk.

Esther fetched a fresh packet of oleomargarine from the icebox. Janet, Joyce, and George Jr. argued over who would squeeze the plastic container until the dark yellow dot in the center was mixed into the white, lard-looking substance to transform it into a pretty yellow. Esther handed the packet to George Jr. He taunted his sisters by deliberately squeezing it slowly as they watched. Finally, the margarine was ready, and they'd all sat down at the table to eat, when Esther felt a twinge in her back.

It couldn't be, she thought. *The baby's not due for a month and a half.*

I knew the story by heart. Each time Mom retold it, I listened to every detail as if I were hearing it for the first time.

"Dr. Lyle never told me he thought you would come early. I decided my back muscles were stretching or you had moved, and I continued eating my breakfast. About five or six minutes later, I felt another pain. I told Joyce I wanted to lie down for a few minutes and asked her to watch the kids. By the time I had the third pain, I knew it wasn't aching muscles; I was going into labor. I asked Joyce to go next door and ask Mrs. Barnett to come over. 'Tell her I'm not feeling well and I need her help.'

"While I waited for her arrival, I thought about Kevin, who had been born two months early. He was born in the hospital, and it had been a very bad experience. I decided I would have you at home.

"Within a few minutes, Mrs. Barnett arrived, and as I was telling her what was happening, my water broke. She sprinted to the phone to call Dr. Lyle. He told her to get a big pot of water boiling and gather some clean towels, and he was on his way.

"You were born about two minutes before he arrived. Joyce was standing on the porch waving her arms and screaming with excitement and yelling, 'My mom had a baby!' when Dr. Lyle stepped out of his car. He ran into the house and found me without taking time to remove his hat.

"He took one look at you and picked up your limp blue body by the heels, held you upside down, and slapped you on the back. You gave out a shrill cry and turned pink.

"Dr. Lyle had just finished everything he had to do when Dad came walking down the dirt driveway carrying some squirrels by their tails. He saw the doctor's car, dropped the squirrels and his gun on the porch, and rushed into the house. Before anyone could say a word, he heard you crying. He just stood there looking at you before he said, 'That's the biggest squirrel I caught today.'

"Dr. Lyle laughed and said, 'She may be bigger than those squirrels you caught but not by a lot. My guess is she weighs four pounds. We need to get her bundled up to keep her warm. Look at her; she's turning blue because she's cold.' Joyce was listening and hurriedly brought a blanket. Dad grabbed a drawer from a dresser, heated some bricks on the kitchen stove, and put them around the outside of the drawer to keep you warm.

"You looked so tiny and sweet lying there. I lay on the sofa watching you until I fell asleep thinking I had the prettiest baby in the whole world. When I woke up, Joyce said she had picked out the name Nancy Lou for you. I didn't know where she came up with that name, but after her many pleas, we decided that would be your name."

When I was eighteen months old, we moved from Minerva, Ohio, to a house my parents rented in Paris, Ohio. It was located in the middle of a dairy farm surrounded by cow pastures and corn, wheat, and hay fields. We were out in the middle of nowhere.

Dad, a brakeman on freight trains, was gone for several days at a time. He parked our old Buick in the train yard in Minerva when he was gone. Mom did not know how to drive. Fortunately, we had everything we needed while he was away. We bought our milk and eggs from the dairy farm owners, and Mom put up a large supply of canned vegetables and potatoes from our garden.

As I grew older, I recognized that my brother Kevin had physical problems. When his development was delayed, Dr. Lyle diagnosed him with cerebral palsy. I watched Dr. Lyle when he came to our house to check Kevin. He would lay him on the kitchen table and show Mom how to exercise his arms and legs. I would stand on my tiptoes and watch Dr. Lyle—and later, Mom—do the exercises several times every day.

It wasn't long before Kevin was strong enough to run and play with the rest of us, although he was clumsy and fell frequently. I had heard Dr. Lyle tell Mom he was not to run because of his bad heart. Even at my young age, I was worried about him and would tell him not to run, but he didn't pay any attention to what I said.

One hot summer day, our family had a scare. My aunt and uncle and their four children were spending the day with us. We were planning on having a wiener roast and homemade ice cream once the sun went down. I was in the kitchen with Mom, Aunt Phyllis, and my cousin Bette, when my brother George came running through the door nearly out of breath and yelling, "A water moccasin bit Raymond."

Our cousins, Raymond and Russell, were about the same ages as my sister Joyce and my brother George. The four of them had been playing outside and wandered off to the creek to catch frogs. Raymond had reached in the water to snatch a frog and pulled his hand out, holding a frog and a water moccasin.

Aunt Phyllis asked, "Where is he?"

"He's way down in the cow pasture. Joyce stayed with him and told me to run and get help. She told Raymond to walk slowly back to the house and suck on the bite to get the venom out."

I got scared. Repeatedly, Dad had cautioned us to be careful when playing at the creek. He'd shown us the water moccasins and told us to remember what they looked like and said they could kill us if we got bit.

That did not stop us from going fishing, swimming, and playing on the banks of the creek. We thought we would be able to see them before it was too late. My city cousins had not been warned. I thought Raymond was going to die.

Mom walked over to the telephone hanging on the wall and turned the crank to reach the operator who would connect her call to Dr. Lyle's office. "My nephew has been bitten by a water moccasin," she said to Dr. Lyle. There was a long silence before I heard her say, "Okay," and she hung up the receiver.

"Dr. Lyle is on his way. He wants Raymond to lie still until he gets here, keep his hand elevated on a pillow, and put some ice on the bite. I have a bag of ice in the icebox that we were going to use to make the ice cream."

Joyce and Raymond got back to the house before Dr. Lyle arrived. Raymond looked scared and pale. He was moaning in pain, and his hand was almost twice its normal size. Aunt Phyllis helped him to lie down on the sofa and told him a doctor was on the way.

Dr. Lyle arrived carrying his black bag. Mom sent me and the other kids to another room, while Dr. Lyle checked Raymond. I put my ear up against the door, straining to hear what they were saying but could only hear muffled sounds.

It seemed like an eternity before Aunt Phyllis walked out of the room and said, "We're going to take Raymond to the hospital. Dr. Lyle gave him antivenin, but he wants him to go to the hospital."

"Is he going to die?" I asked.

"Dr. Lyle said he is going to be okay, but he needs to stay in the hospital for a few days."

Mom stayed busy and didn't have much time to spend with me. Our house did not have electricity. Every day, she had to haul in buckets of coal for the cooking; wood for heating; and water from the well for cooking, bathing, drinking, and washing clothes on the scrub board. Sometimes in the evenings she sat down with us as we listened to stories on our battery-operated radio or we gathered around the old upright piano and sang hymns and silly kids' songs as my mother played the piano.

Instead of relying on Mom, I was helped by my oldest sister, Joyce, in the mornings by brushing and braiding my long hair. We talked as she fixed my hair; I cherished those moments with her. I remember the day she told me I was beautiful and could be Miss America someday. Joyce made me feel special, and I looked up to her and tried to emulate her.

Joyce spent hours cutting out pictures of movie stars from magazines and arranging them in a scrapbook. I decided to make my own scrapbook, but I didn't know the movie stars. I cut out pictures of Van Heusen for my book, to find out it was only an advertisement for a shirt. Joyce explained that the man wearing a shirt was not a movie star; but even more importantly, she didn't laugh at me.

When I was eight years old, Joyce left home to go to nursing school.

I missed her and looked forward to her occasional weekend visits home when I could ask her all about nursing school. She let me look through her textbooks and told me stories about her patients. I would sit for hours at a time looking through her books and listening to her stories.

After Joyce graduated from nursing school, she moved back home and worked at the local hospital. By that time our family had moved to Elyria, Ohio, about seventy-five miles from where we had been living in the country. Before leaving for work, Joyce donned her starched white dress, white nylons, and shiny white Clinic Shoes and carried her white nursing cap with a black stripe in a special hatbox.

If our neighbors had a question about a health problem, they sought her out for advice. I thought about Dr. Lyle's many house calls and now found myself watching Joyce as she helped a neighbor. I made up my mind. I was going to be a nurse, too.

MY FIRST STEP

It was the summer of 1960. Elvis Presley had recently been discharged from the army and had a number one hit, "Stuck On You." John Fitzgerald Kennedy was running for president. Gasoline cost thirty-one cents a gallon. I had just completed a two-week nursing-aide course and was ready to start my first job in a hospital.

Today, I would be reporting for work at Gates Hospital for Crippled Children. I was unfamiliar with the history of this hospital and Elyria Memorial Hospital, which was on the same tract of land. After asking questions, I learned that Elyria, Ohio, did not have an adequate medical facility, prompting some community members to meet on May 28, 1907, to discuss building a hospital. Two days after the meeting, a tragic streetcar accident killed nine passengers and severed passengers' legs and feet. Two of the fatalities were the children of Edgar Allen and Reverend Salsa, members of the hospital committee. The accident provided the momentum to build a thirty-six-bed hospital, which was completed in October 1908.

Shortly after the hospital opened, Edgar Allen began plans to build a crippled children's hospital. Gates Hospital, completed in 1915, was the first hospital in the nation exclusively for the treatment of crippled children. Edgar Allen continued his dedication to providing services by forming the Ohio Society for Crippled Children, the National Society for Crippled Children, and the International Society for Crippled Children, and he also raised funds to establish the Easter Seals Society in 1935. I was awestruck just thinking about my association with this hospital.

My new job paid ninety cents an hour. The past two summers, I had been babysitting for three children, two, five, and nine years old, Monday through Friday, from seven in the morning until five in the evening, earning fourteen dollars a week. At age sixteen, thirty-six dollars a week was music to my ears.

When my alarm sounded, I sprang out of bed to get ready to be at the hospital by seven o'clock. I slipped on my pale green seersucker nursing-aide dress and new white shoes. Mom, who had recently procured her driver's license, drove me to the hospital and dropped me off at the front door. I climbed out of the car, glanced at my reflection in the car window, and thought I looked like a million dollars. My heart was pounding in my chest as I proudly climbed the steps and entered the hospital.

Mrs. Dunfree, the head nurse, greeted me. "I've been looking forward to meeting you. You and Patti Turner, who will be joining us next week, are the first nursing aides to work at Gates Hospital. I don't know exactly what your role will be, but we will figure that out as we go along. Come with me and listen to morning report. Then I'll show you around the hospital."

I followed her to the report room, where I met two nurses and one licensed practical nurse waiting for the report to begin. The night nurse arrived, and we all sat down to listen. The more I listened, the more intimidated I felt hearing medical terms like *triple arthrodesis, Harrington rod, Legg–Calvé–Perthes,* and so on.

I accompanied Mrs. Dunfree to a large ward. Six beds were lined up along one of the walls and facing a row of windows on the opposite side of the room. Three were occupied by young boys who looked like they ranged from seven to ten years old. The wheels at the foot of the beds were resting on eight-inch-high wooden blocks. The boys were lying on boards over their mattresses and slanting down from foot to head by about ten degrees.

8

Each boy had one leg connected to traction secured to his lower leg with an elastic bandage. Ropes emerged from under the bottom edge of the bandage on each side of their ankles and merged together to become a single rope resting on a pulley attached to the foot of the bed. Weights dangled from the ends of the ropes. After staring at the boys for a minute or two, dumbfounded by what I saw, I began looking around the ward.

Hanging over each bed was a trapeze bar suspended above the chest area. Next to each bed were a bedside stand, an over-the-bed table, and a wooden chair. The walls in the room were white and bare. A row of windows let natural light flow into the room, and the main hospital could be seen across the green grassy lawn. There were a piano and some long tables and chairs set up in one area for those who were able come for their meals.

We left the ward and continued our tour by visiting children in their rooms. A child with cerebral palsy was buckled onto a board, allowing him to be in a standing position. A strap secured around his forehead held his head against the board. In a slurred voice he said, "Hello," as I walked into his room. I was deeply moved by the big smile on his face. For the first time, I realized how fortunate my brother Kevin was to have only a mild form of cerebral palsy.

In another room, there was a teenage girl whose leg had been amputated. Farther down the hall was a comatose boy.

Mrs. Dunfree explained, "He was hit by a car six months ago."

"Why is he in this hospital?"

"The staff at Gates can provide range of motion exercises needed to prevent his muscles from atrophying."

Many of the children were polio victims hospitalized to have deformities caused by the disease corrected surgically. The Salk polio vaccine had been discovered several years earlier, so by 1960, active cases of polio were rare. I remembered getting my polio vaccine in 1955, a series of three injections given at one-month intervals. A few years later, the Sabin oral polio vaccine was discovered. I had to be reinoculated by swallowing a sugar cube injected with the vaccine once a month for three months.

There were children in full body casts, lower leg casts and casts that covered entire legs. One cast had old, dried dark brown blood around the ankle area. Through another, bright red blood oozed, with concentric ink marks circled over the bloody area. There was a young boy with a screw

9

going through his lower leg and attached to traction. My stomach flip-flopped as I forced a smile and said, "Hi."

After touring the hospital, I was introduced to Mrs. Stafford, a registered nurse who had worked at Gates Hospital for three and a half years. She was a cheerful young woman in her late twenties. The remainder of my day was spent shadowing her. I fed some of the children, cleaned bedside tables, refilled water pitchers, and tallied intake and output sheets. Near the end of the shift, I played a couple games of checkers with one of the boys.

I left the hospital for the day feeling mentally exhausted, excited, and terrified. Would I be able to care for of these children without doing further harm? That night I dreamed about the children and rolled out of bed early feeling a little less confident.

I was assigned to care for the three boys in traction. They were to be turned on their stomachs for breakfast. I studied the situation, mulling over how to turn them. Unable to figure it out, I sought help. It was simple once I learned all that was necessary was to lift the rope up off the pulley as they flipped over.

After breakfast, I first took care of Dale, the youngest and quietest of the boys. While he was still on his stomach, I got a basin of warm water, washed his backside, and gave him a back rub before turning him on his back to finish his bath. Mrs. Stafford came by when I was done and removed the elastic bandage that held the traction in place. Under the bandage, there were long strips of plastic on each side of Dale's lower leg over the ropes and stockinette. She carefully removed the strips, traction, and stockinette. His skin was wrinkled and red where it had been wrapped. I washed and massaged his leg before Mrs. Stafford sprayed some smelly-sticky adhesive on his leg and reapplied the traction.

It was time to change the sheets. I had practiced making an occupied bed in the nursing-aide course but never with traction and a bed board. It took me twenty minutes just to make Dale's bed. Before moving on to my next patient, I washed the top of Dale's bedside stand, cleaned the drawers, and had everything in place. By eleven in the morning, I had finished with the boys. Before leaving the ward, I surveyed what I had done and felt satisfied and proud.

After lunch, the boys took a nap. Dale's family was in Europe, and no one came to visit with him during afternoon visiting hours.

How sad, I thought. *I'll visit with him.*

I walked into the ward with the visitors, sat down in the chair next to Dale's bed, and asked, "What would you like to do?"

His big brown eyes lit up, and he asked, "Do you know how to play war?"

"That's one of my favorite games."

"Really?"

"Really!"

"Mine too."

"I'm pretty good. Do you want to play?"

"Yeah. I'm good too," he said.

"I'll see if I can find some cards." I got up and returned holding a deck of cards.

We played the game for about an hour before Dale won and proudly announced to the others in the room, "I beat her." They clapped and cheered. Dale looked at me and grinned.

Jokingly, I said, "Just wait until tomorrow."

Eventually, I learned the boys had Legg–Calvé–Perthes disease. For some unknown reason, the body stops supplying an adequate amount of blood to the head of the femur (thigh bone), and the bone dies. The normally round head of the femur can collapse, flatten out, and slip out of its socket in the pelvic bone from standing, walking, or flexing the hip joint. Over time, the blood supply returns to the head of the femur. In the meantime, these children have to stay in traction for a year.

Today, children with Legg–Calvé–Perthes disease are treated on an outpatient basis. If they have severe pain, traction is set up in the home. However, many are able to be up but taught to avoid strenuous activity. They may wear a brace to prevent bending the hip joint.

Once a week, I transported the boys to the tub room on a stretcher for their baths, being careful not to bend the hip joint. When it was Dale's turn, I allowed him to stay in the tub a little longer. He enjoyed the soothing, warm bath more than the other boys and became relaxed and talkative. He was on the verge of tears when he told me, "I miss Dad, Mom, my sister, and my friends."

I had to hold back my tears.

The pace had picked up by the end of the third week. I continued to care for the three boys, and Mrs. Dunfree added Sally and Roger to my assignment.

Sally was a petite, pretty, and vociferous teenager who had polio when she was eight. For half her life, she had been in and out of hospitals and knew exactly what she wanted. She kept her hair neatly combed, demanded a clean gown or sheet if there was a speck of food on it, and had a specific place for every one of her belongings. Sally ordered me around like a drill sergeant. Her spunk was refreshing and demeaning at the same time.

She had had surgery the previous day to realign and stabilize her foot. Following surgery, a cast was applied to her lower leg and foot to hold the newly fused bones in place until they healed. The plaster of Paris cast was damp and heavy. Some light red blood was seeping through the cast at her ankle. Mrs. Stafford checked the amount of blood on the cast every hour and drew a line along the outer edges of the bloodstain with each check to determine how much she was bleeding. She explained, "If the bleeding doesn't show signs of slowing down, I'll need to call the surgeon."

I kept Sally's leg elevated on pillows and placed an ice bag over her ankle to help slow the bleeding and decrease swelling. To reposition her leg on the pillow, I had to lift the heavy cast with the palm of my hand, being careful not to use my fingertips, which could dent the cast, causing pressure areas and skin sores. With the heavy cast balanced in the palm of my hand I used my other hand to fluff and turn over the pillow. I cringed every time Sally screamed in pain and told myself, *It has to be done. I have no choice.*

After three days of using an electric floor fan to dry the cast completely, it was finally ready to be petaled. Mrs. Stafford asked me to "petal" it to keep the edges of the cast dry and prevent small pieces from breaking off and falling into the cast. She had shown me how it was done, yet this was my first attempt.

I carefully cut soft moleskin into equally sized pieces about five inches long and three inches wide. Each piece had a straight bottom and pointed top. Using a tongue blade, I tucked the straight bottom edge down into the cast and folded the top over the outer edge of the cast, slightly overlapping each piece. Once completed, it should have looked like a top of a picket fence. My work looked like an old, rickety fence with uneven picket tops. Sally cried when she saw it, and I felt horrible.

"I will ask Mrs. Stafford to help get this straight," I said. "I am sorry. Yours is the first cast I've petaled. I would cry too if I had to wear something that looked like that."

Sally tried to smile through her tears when Mrs. Stafford came to my rescue and fixed the botched job.

Nine-year-old Roger was also a polio victim and had surgery to lengthen his heel cord. A cast was applied after his surgery, and he complained that it itched under the cast. While cleaning his bedside stand, I found a wire hanger that had been straightened out.

Holding the hanger up where he could see it, I asked, "Where did you get this?"

"One of the girls gave it to me."

"What are you doing with it?"

"I told you, it itches under my cast."

"Did you use it?"

"Yes, and it felt good!"

"I have to throw it away. It is dangerous to stick it down in the cast."

"Please don't," he pleaded.

"I have to. It could cut your skin, and it's a perfect place to get an infection."

Later in the week while helping Roger with his bath, I detected a foul odor. I bent over and sniffed around his cast. That was the source of the stench.

"Roger, have you noticed a strange smell coming from your cast?" I asked.

"Kind of."

"I'm going to have the nurse check it."

Mrs. Stafford validated my suspicions and notified the surgeon, who had been apprised a few days earlier what Roger had done.

Dr. Barrett stopped by in the afternoon. After smelling it for himself, he told Roger, "I'm going to cut a window in your cast to see what's going on."

Roger's eyes filled with terror when the doctor returned to his room brandishing a saw. Dr. Barrett laid the saw on the table and gently patted Roger on this head. "It won't hurt." He plugged in the saw and held it to his skin. "See, it did not cut my skin. This is a magical saw. Does it hurt anywhere under your cast?"

"Right here," Roger said as he pointed to a place on his calf.

Dr. Barrett began cutting out a portion of the cast over the area as Roger held my hand, squeezing it so hard it turned purple. When the doctor lifted out the square piece of cast, the malodor permeated the room. I gasped for air.

After regaining my composure, I looked at the site. Several lacerations oozed a mixture of blood and pus. The skin surrounding the area was bright red and puffy. Dr. Barrett cleaned it, applied Neosporin ointment, and placed gauze dressing over the area. I searched for air freshener. Every day, for two weeks, Mrs. Stafford cleaned the wound, and I sprayed the room. Finally the stench subsided, and the wound healed. Roger promised he would not stick anything down in his cast ever again.

By the end of summer, I felt at ease and loved working with the children. When school was back in session, I made arrangements to work weekends and one evening a week.

Patti Turner and I were scheduled to work a few times on the same night. She was peppy. After dinner, we all sang songs as she played the slightly-out-of-tune upright piano. I played "Chopsticks," the only thing I knew. Once the patients figured out that this was all I knew, they would ask me to play and then laugh and tease me. Because they were having a great time, I did not mind.

During my senior year, I was accepted into the MB Johnson School of Nursing, affiliated with Elyria Memorial Hospital. My classes would begin in the fall.

Following high school graduation, I was ready to work full-time again until I entered nursing school. I was disappointed when I learned there were no full-time nursing-aide positions available at Gates Hospital. Instead, I was offered a full-time job at the Elyria Memorial Hospital Central Supply Department. Without knowing anything about central supply, I accepted the position.

The staff welcomed me and quickly made me feel like I was an important member of the team. I was particularly fond of a licensed practical nurse from Japan, Keiko Barnes, who had married a US serviceman after World War II. She took me under her wing and told me the ins and outs of the department. As a sideline, she taught me how to say good morning, *ohayōu gozaimasu*, and thank you, *arigatō*, in Japanese.

My first chore each morning was cleaning two to three hundred glass thermometers, sent from the nursing care units, by placing them in a large basin filled with lukewarm water and green soap. Keiko told me, "A student nurse put thermometers in hot water and broke all of them."

I remembered her story every time I prepared the water. After the thermometers had soaked for ten minutes, I gently scrubbed each one using a soft-bristle brush. Next, I shook each thermometer with repeated quick snaps of my wrist until the mercury in the thermometer was at or below ninety-four degrees. Finally, I rinsed the thermometers in fresh running cool water, dried them, and laid them on trays for delivery back to the units.

In those days, mercury was not considered a hazardous waste and was thrown away in the general trash. On occasion, when I broke a thermometer, I played with the little ball of mercury before throwing it in the trash can. It was captivating watching the little shiny ball roll around without breaking apart.

The next task was cleaning dirty needles, used for injections, with my bare hands. I placed each needle on a special machine that squirted water through the lumen when the foot plate was pressed. After clearing the lumen of medicine residue, I checked it for burrs by running the tip of the needle across a cotton ball. If the tip snagged the cotton, I sharpened the needle using an Arkansas stone. When the tip no longer snagged cotton, the needle was ready for its final cleaning in hot soapy water. I washed, rinsed, separated them by size, and tucked them into gauze-filled metal containers for the final sterilization process in the autoclave.

Glass syringes had to be washed in a green soap solution, rinsed, dried, and sorted by size. I placed them on metal trays and covered them with a thin cotton towel, before sterilization in the dry heat sterilizer. I was never allowed to operate the dry heat sterilizer or autoclave because special training was required.

My final chore for the morning, one I had fun doing, was cleaning all the gloves. After washing them, I twirled each one to fill it with air, and squeezed the glove until each finger ballooned out. I folded back the top of each glove to form a cuff, matched pairs of gloves by size, wrapped each pair in a green cotton towel, and labeled them according to size before laying them on a tray for dry heat sterilization.

Hundreds of surgical instruments were brought to Central Supply from surgery each day. I was never assigned to clean them; I assume it was because these instruments were expensive and delicate.

In the afternoons, Keiko and I prepared the green cotton drapes used in surgery. We chatted as we stood folding and wrapping the drapes for sterilization. Once that was completed, I set up special trays for urinary catheterizations, spinal taps, and suturing.

The surgical suite was connected to the Central Supply Department. Between surgeries, the surgical staff gathered supplies needed for the next surgery. We kept a file of cards listing all equipment needed for each surgical procedure and notes on each surgeon's special requests for setting up the operating room. I never was allowed to go through the door that led into the surgical suite, and I longed for the day when I could see behind those doors.

In mid-August, I resigned from my nursing-aide job. It was time to start nursing school. The staff threw a party for me and told me I could take anything I wanted from the Central Supply Department as a reminder of my work with them. I was surprised and uncomfortable with their offer, but rather than say anything, I chose to take a thermometer.

My experiences at Gates Hospital and in the Central Supply Department at Elyria Memorial Hospital reinforced my goal to become a nurse. My first love was working with the patients, but I cherished all I had learned in Central Supply. My appetite had been whetted, and I was ready to pursue my dream. I knew, without a doubt, that nursing was my calling.

3

STARTING SCHOOL

I was floating on clouds the day my mother and I attended a welcoming reception in the parlor at the MB Johnson School of Nursing dormitory. When we walked in, several of my future classmates were seated alongside their mothers. I scrutinized everyone in the room, forming opinions based on my first impressions.

Alberta Davis, school director, was an attractive middle-aged woman with silver-gray hair coiffured in a bouffant style with an abundance of hair spray and fashionably dressed. She had a warm, natural smile and walked around the room with a confident, relaxed and upright posture while making eye contact with those near her. Her very presence demanded attention and respect.

Miss Durkin, housemother, was an elderly hunchbacked woman who moved slowly around the room. I had an eerie feeling as I watched her and sensed immediately that she was a woman I would not want to cross.

One of my future classmates, Susan Ujheli, caught my attention with her heavy Southern drawl. I was intrigued listening to her and wondering if she were accentuating the drawl, thinking, *No one really talks like that.*

Another short, red-haired girl, Joanne Schrock, had the best belly laugh. I knew I would like to get to know her better.

Sitting across the room from me was a young girl, Judy Boone, with a sweet, pretty smile that displayed beautiful white teeth. She and I had similar physical features in body shape, height, and weight. One of the big differences, however, was her pretty nose. I never thought my nose as pretty. There was a brand of notebook paper with the profile of an Indian chief on the cover. Each time I purchased a new notebook, I held my face to the cover, and traced the image of my nose next to the Indian chief's nose to show the similarity. I envied Judy's perfectly shaped nose.

I recognized Kate King. We had attended the same high school and had been in only one class together in the four years we were there. She looked different. Her long dark brown, frizzy hair; bucked teeth; and slightly overweight body had been transformed into a thin attractive young woman with a short new hairstyle.

Mrs. Davis gave a welcoming speech, introduced the faculty, and talked about move-in day. I listened intently to everything she had to say.

"All of you have been handpicked. We used new criteria this year. Everyone has an IQ of at least 125. In the past, fewer than half of the students admitted graduated. I expect most of you, if not all, to complete the program."

By the end of her speech, I was eager to get started.

Still all pumped up a week later, I moved into a whole new world. Lugging my suitcases and boxes up four flights of stairs and plopping them on the concrete floor, I paused to look over my surroundings. The small square room was furnished with bunk beds, one desk, two wooden chairs, and two dressers. One window overlooked the front lawn of the dorm.

Shortly after I arrived, Kate King and her mother walked in toting her stuff. I was surprised to have her as my roommate. After a few pleasantries, we picked out our dresser and bed. Kate chose the top bunk, and I felt relieved. As a young child, I had stepped out of a top bunk while sleep walking and had been jolted awake when I'd hit the floor.

Kate's funny and extroverted personality was contrary to my thinking of her as the shy, quiet girl I had imagined from our limited contact. One night after our lights were out, Kate and I could hear loud talking. The voices were coming from outside. Kate slipped out of bed to peer through the window.

"There are four men walking on the lawn. I don't know who they are." She opened our window and said in a deep voice, "This is God speaking. Get the hell off the grass." I would have never contemplated doing anything like that and found it funny and offensive at the same time.

Kate adored her only sibling, an older brother, and spoke of him often. In October 1962, what would come to be known as the Cuban Missile Crisis developed when a reconnaissance mission spotted a Soviet missile base under construction in Cuba. The United States contemplated attacking Cuba, causing a major confrontation and the possibility of a nuclear conflict. Kate became extremely upset, fearing her brother would be drafted into the army and sent to a war zone. She made known her utmost dislike of President Kennedy. My emotions were conflicted because I liked President Kennedy, and my boyfriend, Byron, was in the United States Marine Corps (USMC). Silently I pondered what might happen and secretly loathed Kate's outrage toward our president, yet I appreciated her feelings about losing a loved one in a war.

The school rules were stringent. It was mandatory for all nursing students to live in the dormitory. No males or married persons were allowed in the program, which I assumed was due to lack of accommodations for them.

Curfew for first-year students was at seven o'clock Monday through Thursday and eleven o'clock Friday through Sunday. However, every night, the doors to the dormitory were locked promptly at 11:00 p.m. Any student arriving after that time had to call Miss Durkin to be let in and was automatically grounded for a week. Years later, I learned my classmates returned late and undetected by making prearrangements for a classmate to let them in.

We had an elaborate checkout and check-in system. Each time we left the hospital grounds, we signed out by printing in black ink, indicating the time we were leaving, where we were going, and when we would return. The sign out sheet was designed like a hospital cardex, a form used at the hospital for patient information. Each student had her own form, and our housemother frequently monitored the forms for accuracy and neatness. If we misspelled a word, a single line had to be drawn through the word and "error" with our initials printed above the mistake. We were allowed three errors in thirty days. If we exceeded this number, we were grounded for a weekend.

I took it all in stride, never questioning the purpose and accepting all consequences of my actions.

No males were permitted in our sleeping quarters located on the second through fourth floors of the dormitory. Rooms were available on the main floor for students with male visitors, but the doors had to be kept open at all times. Miss Durkin roamed the hall when the rooms were in use.

Interns and residents from foreign countries, with wives and families back in their home country, worked at the hospital. Some asked students out for a date, lying about their marital status, apparently unaware that a list of the names of those who were married was posted on the dormitory bulletin board.

First-year students were expected to be in their rooms studying from seven until nine in the evening. Miss Durkin made rounds at least once during study times to assure we were in our rooms studying. Kate occasionally kept a novel in her textbook to read during study times that, to my surprise, Miss Durkin never noticed.

The school of nursing supplied our student uniforms, nursing caps, and wool capes. The hospital laundry washed, starched, and ironed our uniforms every week.

Each uniform included a blue dress with an attached stiff white collar and cuffs, a white apron, and a bib. Studs fastened the bib to the apron in the front and back and closed the apron at the waist. We were lucky since this was the first year the collars and cuffs were attached. Prior to that, students attached them with studs. Our aprons were to be folded over on our laps while we were sitting. Until we got organized and more adept at putting our uniform together, it took about twenty minutes just to get dressed.

Our white nylons were held up with a garter belt or girdle, and we wore white shoes. Each evening, I polished and shined my leather lace-up Clinic Shoes and washed the laces every week. Byron "spit-shined" my shoes when he made occasional trips home for a weekend. I wore them in pride, thinking they were the best-looking shoes in the entire hospital.

All our meals were served in the hospital cafeteria, and we were expected to eat three meals a day. Meal cards for each student were kept in a holder at the entrance to the cafeteria. We handed our meal card to a dietary staff member, who initialed it to indicate we had shown up for our meal. The food tasted good at first, but it was the same menu over and over again. It wasn't long before we joined our classmates in singing, "Oh, the biscuits that they give us they say are mighty fine; one rolled off the table and killed a friend of mine. I don't want no more of nursing life; gee, Mom, I wanna go home."

It was necessary for us to learn hospital etiquette before going to our first assignment at the hospital. When entering an elevator, we were to wait for a doctor to enter first, and once he was in the elevator, we could board. If the elevator stopped at a floor and a doctor was there to get on, we had to step out of the elevator, allow the physician to enter, and then reenter if there was room.

When doctors walked into the nursing station, we were required to stand. If no chairs were available, we had to give them our chairs and any patient charts they needed. Ironically, in the classroom, we were taught that nursing was a profession. Yet what we were required to do seemed like a contradiction.

Patients, staff, students, and doctors were addressed as Mr., Mrs., Miss, or Dr. First names were not permitted. This was so deeply ingrained that, one weekend when a group of my classmates went to Cleveland to be on *The Mike Douglas Show*, all introduced themselves as Miss with their last names. I had gotten sick and was not able to accompany them but watched them on television that morning. I could see that Mike was trying to get them to give their first name as he circled their table with his microphone, and I was saying as I watched, "Come on—tell him your first name." No one did.

During our freshman year, we were bussed two days a week to Oberlin College for our anatomy and physiology, chemistry, microbiology, sociology, psychology, and nutrition courses. We sang songs the upperclassmen taught us that had been passed down to them when they were freshman. Riding the bus was our cue to sing our theme song: "I'm from MBJ so pity me. There's not a man in this damn nunnery. And every night at four, they bolt the door. I don't know what the hell I ever came here for ..."

We used techniques taught to us by the older students to memorize specific information. The acrostic "on old Olympia's towering top a Fin and German vaulted a hedge" was used to remember the cranial nerves. And "Never lower Tilley's pants; Mother might come home," helped to jog our recall of the wrist bones.

Our nutrition instructor was elated about a major breakthrough in genetic coding. It had been discovered that ribonucleic acid, RNA, was a double helix. I could not comprehend why she was so excited about this finding except that she called it "solving the mystery of life." Eventually I understood this discovery was a link to evolution.

Early in the morning on test days, while my classmates slept, I crawled out of bed and went to the small kitchen in the dormitory to study. It was a quiet space where I could concentrate, even though I hated getting up so early. During those wee morning hours, I learned to enjoy a hot cup of coffee.

In our Fundamentals of Nursing course, we studied and practiced various procedures—making occupied and unoccupied beds, giving baths and back rubs, applying bandages, binders and compresses, collecting specimens, taking vital signs, preparing and giving enemas, preparing medications, and caring for patients in isolation. My favorite procedure was receiving a soothing backrub; my least favorite was enduring an enema.

While learning these skills, we were taught good body mechanics to prevent back injuries. Hospital beds were high, so bending was not necessary while caring for patients. Footstools were used to get patients in and out of bed, since the entire bed could not be lowered. Only the head and foot of the bed could be adjusted up or down using cranks with hinges that allowed the crank to be swiveled under the bed when not in use. It took bruising my legs several times before remembering to push the crank out of the way.

Learning these skills was exacting. When practicing making beds, stress was placed on them being wrinkle-free, since most patients spent the majority of their time in bed. There were no fitted bottom sheets, so a flat sheet was placed on the bed with the seams facing down to prevent irritating the patient's skin. A rubber draw sheet and a muslin draw sheet were pulled tightly across the middle of the bed. A top sheet was placed with seams facing up. When it was turned back over the bedspread the seam did not show. Next, the bedspread was added with the seam facing down. We practiced making mitered corners until they passed inspection. A toe pleat in the top covers allowed wiggle room for the patient's toes to prevent foot drop and provide comfort. Lastly, the pillow was placed with the pillowcase opening facing away from the doorway for aesthetic purposes. The linens passed the instructor's tightness test if a quarter bounced on them.

Our tools for work were a wristwatch with a second hand, a pair of bandage scissors, and a pen that we carried in our uniform pockets. Only since the 1950s were nurses allowed to use a stethoscope. I heard doctors were rebuked for teaching nurses how to use them and were warned that nurses would get into trouble for having too much knowledge. We used the stethoscope only while checking blood pressures and fetal heart rates. Even the use of a thermometer had been contested before nurses were actually permitted to use one. Gloves were limited to working in the operating room or isolation room and inserting a urinary catheter.

After hours of laboratory practice, we were ready to use our newly learned skills on actual patients. We were not assigned to do the total care of a patient at the hospital but to perform the skills we knew. For example, once we learned how to do vital signs, we checked vital signs on patients, which included taking oral and rectal temps, counting pulses and respirations, checking blood pressures, and charting our findings in the patients' charts. Our instructor went with us for the first few times until she was satisfied we could do them accurately. While I was counting a pulse, she counted it on the patient's other wrist. When I checked a blood pressure, we used a special stethoscope with two earpieces, so she could listen in.

One morning, I was assigned to take vital signs, feeding, bathing, and making the bed for Mr. Pappas, a middle-aged man with a brain tumor. He stared at me with his large protruding dark eyes as I moved about in his room. There was a spooky quietness during his bath, since he was unable to speak. I tried to concentrate on what I was doing, but my thoughts wandered to thinking of impending death. As I reached out to turn him on his side, he suddenly grabbed my breasts. I stood there startled for a second or two before grabbing his wrists and taking his hands off me. I chose not to say anything, thinking he couldn't comprehend that what he had done was wrong. For the remainder of the morning, I kept close vigilance on his hands at all times while at his bedside.

Early one morning, as I was finishing making my patient's bed, Mrs. Davis walked into the room. She looked clean and fresh in her white lab coat, whereas I felt dingy and sweaty after helping my patient get out of bed and then making the bed. Mrs. Davis looked over the bed I had just made with a nod of approval, but her expression changed when she glanced at my shoes. "Don't you know how to tie shoes?" she asked.

Somewhat puzzled, I looked down at my shoelaces, which were tied, and answered, "Yes."

"The bow should go across the shoe, not up and down the shoe," she explained. "Watch me as I show you how to tie shoes properly," she said as she bent over to tie my shoe. When she finished, the bow went across my shoe, but I couldn't see what she had done differently from the way I had been tying them.

"How did you do that?" I asked. She did a repeat demonstration before I tried to tie my shoelace with her watching. After I retied it, the bow went up and down the shoe again. "Why does my bow do that?" I asked, feeling quite humiliated.

"You're putting the shoelace under the loop you made. Try putting it over the loop," she explained.

I tried doing it her way, and, lo and behold, the bow went across my shoe. "Wow, that is probably the first time I ever had my bow right."

Mrs. Davis had a slight smirk on her face as she walked out of the room.

I looked at my patient, who had been watching the whole scenario, and said, "All these years I never noticed my shoelaces weren't tied right."

My patient chuckled, and I felt a little less embarrassed.

The bedpans and urinals were made of shiny stainless steel, cold to the touch. We were taught to warm a bedpan by swishing hot water around in the pan before placing it under a patient. One of my classmates warmed her patient's urinal before handing it to him. Word traveled quickly, and the staff, her patient, and classmates teased her ruthlessly. Back at the dorm, Joanne, our belly laugher, could be heard above all the others combined.

Full bedpans and urinals were carried to the dirty utility room for cleaning. Before walking down the hall with a bedpan or urinal, we covered it with a blue-and-gray striped, heavy cotton cloth made specifically for that purpose. Everyone knew what we were carrying as we emerged from a room with the blue-and-gray cover.

The urinals were rinsed with cold water, since hot water intensified the urine odor. Bedpans were placed in a special device called a hopper, which flushed, sprayed, washed, and steamed them. The bedpans were hot and shiny when removed from the hopper and taken back to the patient's room, ready for the next "go."

Several days before I had the opportunity to use a hopper, my instructor demonstrated the correct way to place the bedpan in the hopper. The problem was, I could not remember the precise details. Did the bedpan go in the hopper right side up or upside down? I decided to turn the bedpan upside down while placing it in the hopper. Mistake! The door to the hopper was not sealed tightly, and a mixture of water and urine sprayed all over me. I had to return to the dorm to shower and change my uniform before continuing with my work.

Near the end of our first year, *Ben Casey* and *Dr. Kildare* were popular new television shows. Watching them became a top priority. Two evenings a week, we congregated in the TV room, trying to guess the diagnosis of each patient before it was revealed and criticizing the TV doctors. We debated on which MD was smarter and more handsome. Even though Dr. Ben Casey's pronunciation of medical terms was horrific, half the class voted for him. His exceedingly good looks absolved him of all faults. Dr. Kildare won the hearts of the other half.

A few months before the end of our first year, our family and friends were invited to our capping ceremony held at The First Congregational Church. Each nursing school had its own unique cap design identifying the wearer's alma mater. After Mrs. Davis delivered a speech, one by one, our names were called. We walked to the center of the stage to receive our caps, which were then pinned onto our heads by our nursing instructor. The cap was all white with one black velvet stripe. The one stripe indicated we were first year students. Each year, we would be given another stripe to add to our cap. We adhered the stripes to our caps using a thin strip of white toothpaste that we smoothed out on the underside of the stripe before carefully pressing it on our cap. Before we took our place on the stage, we were given a Florence Nightingale lamp that held a small white candle.

Once the capping was completed, we lit our candles. The lights in the auditorium were turned low. In the darkness, we took our oath by reciting the Nightingale pledge in unison. The pledge was first used in 1893 and was the first code of ethics for nurses. It reads:

> I solemnly pledge myself before God and in the presence of this assembly, to pass my life in purity and to practice my profession faithfully. I will abstain from whatever is deleterious and mischievous, and will not take or knowingly administer any harmful drug. I will do all in my power to maintain and elevate the standard of my profession, and will hold in confidence all personal matters committed to my keeping and all family affairs coming to my knowledge

in the practice of my calling. With loyalty will I endeavor to aid the physician, in his work, and devote myself to the welfare of those committed to my care.

Our caps had a fairly simple design. They looked like a short fat T before they were folded with small buttonholes that lined up when pleated so studs could be placed through them to hold the pleats together. The hospital laundry washed and starched our caps before sending them back for us to fold.

After graduation, I had to wash and starch my cap. Once my cap was washed, I put it in full-strength starch and plastered it to the refrigerator door to dry. I ran my hands over the cap many times to get the excess starch out, making it smooth. Twenty-four hours later, when the cap was completely dry, I peeled it off the refrigerator door. It was as stiff as a piece of cardboard and ready to be folded.

When we entered our second year, we carried on the traditions of dormitory life. As a prank, we made sign-up sheets for shower times and posted them on the wall in the shower room. The new group of students were deluged with so many rules they never suspected the shower times were a ruse. We watched with amusement as each girl would suddenly excuse herself from a conversation or some other activity to whisk off for her allotted fifteen-minute shower time. The gig was up after a week or two when our ploy was exposed.

Our evening curfew hours were extended to nine o'clock Monday through Thursday, midnight on Friday and Saturday, and eleven on Sunday. Even with these extended hours, it seemed that we were rarely out until curfew. The school had accomplished its mission of helping us develop good study habits.

A few classmates went out one evening and returned drunk. That was the first time I had seen someone inebriated. I was in the bathroom when the girls came in laughing, and one of them came out of the toilet stall with her shorts soaked in urine. She had not pulled them down before urinating and was oblivious to her condition. She walked out of the bathroom laughing, not stopping to wash her hands. I thought it was disgusting.

During the week, some of the girls dated. Joanne had been dating Joseph and could be heard singing, "I want to be Joey's girl. I want to be

Joey's girl. That's the most important thing to me," a parody on a popular hit, "Bobby's Girl."

My boyfriend was in the USMC and was away on cruises for three or more months at a time. We corresponded by mail nearly every day, and on rare occasions, he returned home for a weekend. When he was on a cruise, the mail did not arrive regularly. For a week or two, my mailbox would be empty and then, voila, an avalanche of letters would surface.

By the beginning of our third and final year in the program, about a third of the girls were engaged, with more anticipated engagements to come. Sunday evenings when I returned to the dorm, I would borrow one of my classmates' rings and announce that I had gotten engaged. I never fooled them.

Saturday, September 21, 1963, the day before my twentieth birthday, I received a birthday card from Byron, who was on a Mediterranean cruise. I opened the envelope, and a diamond ring fell out. I grabbed the ring and ran upstairs so my mother wouldn't see it.

I sat down on my bed and read the card, which said, "I bought you something for your birthday, but I forgot to punch holes in the box, and it died." Handwritten at the bottom of the card was "Will you marry me? Don't worry, it's real."

I slipped the ring on my finger. It was beautiful and fit perfectly. The whole time my mother had been yelling to me and asking, "Are you okay?"

I was shaking as I took the ring off, and clenching it in my hand, I walked downstairs. "Do you want to see what Byron sent in my birthday card?" I asked as I held out my clenched fist.

"What is it?" she asked.

Slowly I opened my shaking hand. My mother gazed at it for a second or two before asking, "Are you going to keep it?"

I hadn't considered that question. "I don't know. I wasn't expecting this," I responded.

After pondering her question for a few minutes, I slipped the ring back on my finger. My mother got all excited and couldn't get to the phone fast enough to tell her friends. I was in love—with Byron and nursing.

MEDICAL-SURGICAL NURSING

Our instructor, Miss Brown, greeted us with "Shut up and open a window." She walked briskly, carrying an armload of books, and plopped them on her desk. "Stand up and do ten jumping jacks." She began counting, "One, two, three"; stopped; and shouted, "Get moving!" We hopped to our feet and began jumping.

I thought, *She sure is zippy for an old woman.*

Her eyes, framed with crow's feet, sparkled with a hint of mischievousness, wrinkles were etched deeply in her cheeks, and blond hairs peeked through the gray.

"Before you graduate, some of you will surmise you have appendicitis, gallbladder disease, a brain tumor, or some rare disease."

We laughed.

Wagging her finger at us, she said, "It happens in every class."

A few days later she added to her habitual greeting, "And, Miss Johnson, sit up."

The door to the classroom was located behind us. One morning, we opened a window, taped our mouths shut with masking tape, and reminded Karen Johnson to sit up straight.

Miss Brown arrived shouting, "Shut up; open a window; and, Miss Johnson, sit up!"

Upon reaching the front of the room and turning to face us, she burst into laughter. The next day, she made her grand entrance with the usual greeting.

Mr. Jenkins was hospitalized with congestive heart failure. He was receiving digoxin 0.25 mg every morning, and I was going to give it. In Fundamentals of Nursing, we studied basic pharmacology, where I learned the five Rs—right medicine, right dose, right route, right time, and right patient. The apothecary, metric, and household systems were taught as well. I learned how to convert from one system to another. The information was stored in my head, ready to be put into action. Numbers were bouncing around in my brain—fifteen grains in a gram, sixty milligrams in a grain, thirty milliliters in an ounce, five milliliters in a teaspoon, one thousand milligrams in a gram, one thousand grams in a kilogram, and on and on and on.

Before administering the digoxin, I had to complete an index card about the drug with indications for use, dosage range, side effects, possible adverse reactions, toxicity, and contraindications for use. After completing the card, I put it in the empty file box I'd brought with me to the hospital. That box became one of my nursing tools.

My instructor Miss Slusser and I went to the medication room. Hanging on the wall was a medication cardholder with twenty-four pockets, one for each hour of the day. Physicians wrote medication orders in patients' charts. The head nurse transcribed the orders by making a medication card with the patient's name, name and dose of medication, route of delivery, and times the medication was to be given and put it in the cardholder under the appropriate time. I found Mr. Jenkins's card for digoxin in the 8:00 a.m. pocket and began preparing his medication by finding a bottle of digoxin tablets labeled 0.25 mg in a cabinet.

The questioning began. "Why is your patient getting digoxin?"

"He has congestive heart failure. It will strengthen his heart contractions."

"What is the normal dosage range?"

I pulled out my index card. "It's 0.25 to 0.75 mg."

"What are the reasons for withholding the medicine?"

"Pulse below sixty or a big drop in his usual heart rate."

"What has his pulse been running?"

"It was eighty-two this morning and has been running in the eighties to low nineties."

"What are the symptoms of toxicity?"

Reading from my index card I said, "Loss of appetite; nausea; vomiting; diarrhea; slow, irregular, or sudden drop in heart rate; headache; confusion; drowsiness; and blurred vision."

I poured one pill into the cap of the bottle without touching it, dumped it in a paper soufflé cup, and placed it with my card on a small tray. Before putting the bottle back, I rechecked the dose written on the card two times, fulfilling the requirement of checking a dose three times. I was ready.

Miss Slusser and I walked down the hall to Mr. Jenkins's room. My cherished dream was becoming a reality. It was exhilarating. I gave the medication without a hitch and charted it as "given" before returning the medication card to the 8:00 a.m. cardholder pocket. I saw two RNs preparing medicines for their patients and noticed some cups contained multiple pills. Immediately, I asked myself, "How will I remember which med is which in the cup? What if I have to withhold a pill?" I asked my instructor about this dilemma.

"You will recognize the pills after you've given them over and over again."

I wasn't fully convinced.

Mrs. Lance had a duodenal ulcer, believed at the time to be caused by the production of too much hydrochloric acid. Treatment was based on the belief that stress and poor dietary habits (eating spicy foods, consuming alcohol, and skipping meals) were the root cause.

Mrs. Lance's orders included bed rest to relieve stress and a Sippy diet—a diet used in the initial stages of treatment of an ulcer to decrease hydrochloric acid production. Every hour, on the hour, I gave Mrs. Lance three ounces of half-and-half, and every hour, on the half hour, one ounce of Maalox. By noon Mrs. Lance faked gagging when I appeared in her room with the dreaded white liquid.

"How long do I have to drink this stuff?"

"In two and a half days, the frequency will decrease, and you'll get a soft-boiled egg three times a day."

Sarcastically, she said, "I can't wait."

Patting her shoulder and handing her the Maalox, I said, "Bottoms up."

She puckered her lips, took the cup, and began sipping slowly.

A few days after getting soft-boiled eggs, cream of wheat, and mashed potatoes, Mrs. Lance announced, "I'm getting hungry for real food, something that tastes good. Spaghetti with lots of Parmesan cheese would be marvelous."

"You must be feeling better, but that's too spicy. It would aggravate your ulcer."

"Not getting good food aggravates my ulcer!"

Several days later, Mrs. Lance received a modified bland diet and Maalox four times a day. The half-and-half was discontinued.

"My stomach hasn't hurt for two days. Dr. Lautenschleger said I could go home tomorrow if I don't start having pain again. Say a prayer for me."

"I will. What are you going to do when you get home?"

"Have a good home-cooked meal."

"With lots of spices?"

"I won't spice it up too much."

"Would you tell Dr. Lautenschleger if you had pain?"

"I wouldn't lie."

"Good."

Mrs. Lance was discharged with instructions to remain on a bland diet for the rest of her life. Six months later, she was readmitted to the hospital with the same problem and began the Sippy diet.

Nearly ten years later, endoscopies were performed to visualize and biopsy ulcer sites. Drs. Robin Warren and Barry Marshall found large amounts of *Helicobacter pylori* bacteria and proposed using antibiotics to cure ulcers. The medical community did not believe bacteria could survive in an acidic environment, dismissed the discovery, and continued to treat patients with the same regimen. Today, duodenal ulcers are treated with antibiotics.

If Mrs. Lance had been treated with antibiotics the ulcer would have been cured and its return would have been unlikely.

Two nights ago, eighteen-year-old Mr. Adams came to the emergency room complaining of severe abdominal pain. Dr. Massey performed an emergency appendectomy. Unfortunately, Mr. Adams's appendix burst before it could be removed. The infected material spilled into his abdominal cavity, causing peritonitis, a potentially fatal infection. He was receiving intramuscular injections of penicillin every four hours.

In the nursing lab, I practiced giving injections. I was comfortable and confident giving shots to an orange. Today, my comfort level was plummeting.

Miss Slusser found me. "I'm ready to watch you prepare Mr. Adams's penicillin."

"Me too. Let's get it over with."

"Gather everything you need."

Using sterile forceps, I grasped a glass syringe and plunger from a tray and pushed the plunger into the syringe.

Looking at the canisters of needles, Miss Slusser asked, "What size needle are you going to use?"

"A 20-gauge, two and a half inch."

"Good choice."

I pulled a needle from the canister with forceps and fastened it on the syringe tip. Surprisingly, my hands were steady. They sure didn't match the way my stomach felt.

"Is the penicillin kept in the refrigerator?"

"No. It's in the cabinet labeled 'parenteral meds,'" replied Miss Slusser.

I found a vial of crystalline penicillin with the dosage I needed. There was a white powder in the bottle.

Miss Slusser said, "Read the label for instructions on how to reconstitute it."

I read the label and said, "I need to inject two milliliters of sterile saline in the bottle and roll it in my hands until the contents are clear."

"Use the needle and syringe you have to draw up the saline and put it in the bottle of penicillin. Be sure to clean the tops of both bottles with alcohol."

There were jars of cotton balls soaking in alcohol. I had reached for the jar when Miss Slusser said, "Let the alcohol dry before you stick the needle through the rubber top. Don't blow on it."

She was beginning to get on my nerves. I knew that. Blowing on it would recontaminate the vial tops. It took two minutes of rolling the bottle before the powder completely dissolved. I drew up the medicine, procured a fresh alcohol-soaked cotton ball and was ready to go to Mr. Adams's room.

"Where are you going to give the medicine?" she inquired.

"In his buttock."

"Why?"

"The muscle is larger. I think it would irritate the muscle in his arm. Besides, he won't be able to see what I'm doing," I said half laughing.

She smiled and asked, "How will you avoid hitting the sciatic nerve?"

"I'll divide his buttock into four quadrants and use the upper outer quadrant for the injection site."

"Good. You're ready. Let's go."

Mr. Adams was lying on his back with his eyes closed. He looked so peaceful. I hated to disturb him. The night nurse reported he was awake most of the night with a fever, nausea, vomiting, and pain. She had given him medication to help him get some rest.

"Mr. Adams."

He opened his eyes.

"I'm sorry I have to awaken you, but it's time for your penicillin. Do you need help rolling over?"

He shook his head, moaned, and rolled on his side.

I checked his wristband and said, "Tell me your name."

"You know who I am."

"I know, but I need to have you tell me. It's an extra precaution. I don't want to give medicine to the wrong person."

"Richard Adams."

"Thanks."

I partitioned off his buttocks with imaginary lines and swiped the injection site with the cotton ball. Using one hand, I pulled the skin taut and, with my other hand, thrust the needle through his skin into muscle with one quick motion. The needle went in much easier than it did through orange skin. I pulled back on the plunger. When no blood returned, I pushed the plunger. It wouldn't budge. I pushed harder.

Nothing happened. Exasperated, I looked up at my instructor. A ball of sweat trickled down my brow.

Miss Slusser mouthed the words, "Take it out," while making a hand gesture to pull the needle out. I pulled it out, and we walked back to the medication room.

"What happened?"

"The penicillin crystallized in the syringe." She picked up the syringe and tried to push the plunger. "It's as hard as a rock. Throw it away."

"Why did that happen?"

"I don't know. It just happens."

"Is there anything I can do to guarantee it won't happen again?"

"No."

I repeated the whole procedure, this time with heightened anxiety, and returned to Mr. Adams's room.

"Mr. Adams, I have to give your penicillin again. It wouldn't go into your muscle the first time."

"Why?"

"It hardened in the syringe."

He muttered, "What else can go wrong?"

Exactly my sentiments! I gave the injection and rubbed the site with a cotton ball.

"Are you done?"

"Yes. No problem this time," I said, picking up my tray and leaving the room.

"You're good to go," said Miss Slusser. "I won't need to observe you give him his next injection."

"Thanks. It was a nerve-racking experience. I'm glad you were with me."

I was caring for two acutely ill patients—Mr. Dempsey, who'd had a myocardial infarction (heart attack) two days ago, and Mr. Stang, a newly diagnosed diabetic.

My nerves were on edge, so I told Miss Slusser, "I'm apprehensive caring for two patients. Things could go sour quickly."

"The staff nurses will check your patients throughout the day."

I checked in with Mr. Dempsey. "How are you feeling this morning?"

"Tired. I had trouble sleeping. There was too much noise. This bed is uncomfortable, and I had chest pain. The nurse gave me a shot of morphine, and I slept for about an hour."

"Are you having any chest pain now?"

"No, none since the morphine shot."

"That sounds good. Is there anything you need before I leave?"

"I would like some water."

I poured some water in a cup and held it for him to sip some through the straw.

"I like cold water. Could you get some ice?"

"No ice. Doctors orders."

"Just a little won't hurt."

"Cold drinks make blood vessels constrict. Keeping the heart muscle arteries dilated promotes healing.

"Just a few sips?"

"That's my understanding."

He drank the room temperature water.

"Would you like to be turned on your side?"

"Yes. My back is aching."

I rolled Mr. Dempsey on his side and propped his back with pillows. "I'll see you in about thirty minutes."

I left his room and walked down the hall to meet my other patient.

"Good morning, Mr. Stang. My name is Miss Swan. I'll be taking care of you today."

"I want to go home and back to work. I don't have any vacation time or insurance."

"I saw that you have a wife and six-month-old baby. You need to stay and get better so you can get back to work."

"I'm not going to get better. My grandfather had diabetes. He died from it."

"Treatment has improved. We can get your blood sugar back to normal and teach you and your wife how to manage your diabetes. What do you know about diabetes?"

"I could have a heart attack, go blind, lose a foot, or die."

"I've heard stories like that, but I'm learning treatment is continually improving, and complications have decreased significantly."

At one time, diabetes was considered a death sentence. Children died within weeks of diagnosis, and adults within months to a few years. In 1500 BC, the first recorded mention of diabetes in an Egyptian text described it as a mysterious disease that attracts ants and flies to the person's urine. In AD 250, the Greeks named the disease diabetes, meaning "to siphon." They had observed the symptoms of thirst and frequent urination. The Romans added mellitus, meaning "honey-sweet," to the name in AD 500. "Water tasters" literally tasted urine to make the diagnosis of diabetes mellitus.

Diabetes was treated initially with exercise. Later, physicians realized dietary changes could help manage diabetes. In 1922, insulin was used for the first time to successfully treat a teenager.

Mr. Stang had been a seemingly healthy young man who, in spite of his increased appetite, was losing weight and getting weaker. His wife noticed his insatiable thirst and appetite, frequent trips to the bathroom, and weight loss. She encouraged him to see a doctor, which he kept putting off, until yesterday when he began having trouble seeing and couldn't muster up enough energy to go to work. Dr. Koch recognized the symptoms of diabetes immediately and sent him straight to the hospital with orders.

"Did you have a lab test this morning?"

"They took some blood."

"Good. I need to test your urine," I said as I handed him the urinal.

"What is that for?"

"To check the amount of sugar and acetone in your urine. Dr. Koch will let us know how much insulin to give you based on all the test results."

"How many shots am I going to get?"

"Two this morning—one long-acting and one short-acting insulin. We will be testing your urine three more times today, and you will receive short-acting insulin each time. You won't need the short-acting insulin when there is no sugar or acetone in your urine."

"That's good. I'm a construction worker and get covered in dirt. I wouldn't be able to get shots at work. How long is this going to take? I need to get back home and make some money."

"Let's see how each day goes."

I took the urine sample to the dirty utility room. Miss Slusser arrived to supervise the testing and watched as I gathered the Clinitest and Acetest tablets, a glass test tube, and a medicine dropper.

I read aloud the instructions printed on the box of Clinitest tablets before putting the specified number of drops of water and urine and the Clinitest tablet into the test tube. I looked at my watch and began timing thirty seconds.

The tablet began to fizz, and the test tube got hot. I thought I was going to drop it before switching my grip to the top of the tube.

"The instructions forgot to say the test tube gets hot," I said.

Miss Slusser smiled and said, "You won't forget how to hold the test tube next time."

Smarty-pants, I muttered to myself.

After thirty seconds, I gently shook the test tube and compared the color of the solution with the color chart on the box. The solution was bright orange, indicating a "4+" sugar level in the urine, the highest amount that could be detected using this method.

Next, I laid the white Acetest tablet on a paper towel and put one drop of urine on the tablet. Following the instructions on the box, I waited fifteen seconds before comparing the color of the tablet with the color chart. The dark purple tablet matched up with the color for a "large" amount of acetone present in the urine.

Acetone is formed when the body breaks down fats for energy. This happens if a person is starving or, in Mr. Stang's case, has a lack of insulin to break down carbohydrates (glucose) for energy.

Miss Slusser instructed me to chart the results and give them to the head nurse so insulin orders could be obtained. Dr. Koch was in the nursing station with the patient's chart. I gave him the test results. He wrote the insulin orders, and the head nurse made medication cards and handed them to me.

Mr. Stang was ready for breakfast after he had his insulin. He held up the piece of paper from his tray and struggled to read what it said. "What is this? One thousand and eight hundred cal ADA?"

"The name of your special diet, an eighteen hundred-calorie American Diabetes Association diet. You'll receive 1,800 calories a day with specific amounts of food from each food group."

"Oh. I'm glad I don't have to figure that out."

"That will come later."

His eyes filled with tears, and he avoided eye contact.

Feeling like an ogre, I said, "Go ahead and eat before your insulin kicks in."

I went back to my other patient, Mr. Dempsey. He was still propped on his side. His breakfast tray was sitting on his bedside table.

"I'm back. Are you ready for breakfast?"

"Yes, it smells good."

I rolled him on his back and cranked up the head of the bed. "You're on a two-gram low-sodium diet, but you can use this salt substitute if it tastes too bland," I said as I held up the packet.

I gave him some eggs.

"They would taste better with some salt and pepper on them."

I sprinkled the salt substitute and pepper on his eggs and gave him another bite. "Is that better?"

"Much better."

"After lunch, I am going to meet with the dietician and plan your meals for tomorrow. What do you like to drink with your meals?"

"Coffee and juice at breakfast. Milk for lunch and supper."

"Are there any foods you don't like?"

"Let me think." Mr. Dempsey contemplated for a few seconds. "I don't like Brussels sprouts, asparagus, or rutabagas."

"It's a deal. By the way, I wouldn't have chosen the Brussels sprouts or rutabagas. They make me gag."

We both laughed.

All student nurses met with a dietician to plan the menus for their patients who were on special diets, and over time, I became proficient at planning any type of diet.

Mr. Dempsey was on complete bed rest. He was not allowed to bathe, feed, shave, brush his teeth, or turn over. There wasn't anything for him to do except rest, sleep, think, worry, and wait for someone to show up to care for his basic needs.

We talked while I fed him. He was fifty-three years old; had a wife, three grown children, and two grandchildren; and had worked at the *Chronicle Telegram*, the local newspaper, since high school graduation.

Mr. Dempsey was congenial. He didn't have the type A personality I had been told characterized most men with heart attacks—demanding, competitive, hardworking, and impatient. He confided in me, admitting he was scared and adding, "My father dropped over dead from a heart attack when he was sixty."

"I'm sorry to hear that. In your case, I don't think the saying 'like father, like son' applies. You have survived the most critical time, the first hour."

"But I had chest pains last night."

"That is common following a heart attack. You did the right thing by telling your nurse and getting pain medicine."

Following breakfast, I gave Mr. Dempsey a bath and back rub, brushed his teeth, combed his hair, shaved him, and changed his sheets. By the time I finished, he was ready to take a nap.

I returned to Mr. Stang's room. He was staring at the ceiling.

"I'm back. I'll get a basin of water so you can get washed."

After taking his bed bath, Mr. Stang sat in a chair while I made his bed. He asked, "How long will I be in the hospital?"

Thinking, *He isn't going to let this go*, I hesitated before saying, "I'm not sure. Maybe one to two weeks."

"I can't stay that long. I have got to get back to work. When I'm not working, there's no money."

"When your doctor comes in, tell him that you have to get back to work. In the meantime, we'll teach you and your wife how to test your urine, give insulin shots, and plan your meals."

Mr. Stang proved to be a quick learner, and by the end of the week, he was able to test his urine and give himself insulin injections. The hospital dietician met with him and his wife, and together they were beginning to plan menus according to the ADA guidelines. Mr. Stang would be ready for discharge as soon as his blood sugar was stabilized.

Mr. Dempsey remained on complete bed rest. Each morning and afternoon, I did passive range of motion exercises to improve circulation to his legs. He remained in the hospital for five more weeks, and even though I wasn't assigned to take care of him, I stopped by to say hello each time I was on the unit. I was there on his day of discharge and joined in the celebration.

For the next few weeks, each time I was at work, I thought about Mr. Dempsey and wondered how he was managing at home. It would probably be a full year before his doctor released him to return to his job.

It was a hot summer day with the temperature nearing ninety degrees. Miss Slusser decided to send a couple of my classmates and me to observe our first autopsy. We went down to the hospital basement in search of the morgue. There was a long hall with people seated on wooden benches lined up against both sides, waiting to be seen in the outpatient clinic. The patients were fanning themselves, and drops of sweat were beginning to roll down my forehead.

Miss Slusser led us into the morgue through an unmarked door between two of the benches and directed us to stand in a line along a wall. We had an unobstructed view of the shiny steel table in the center of the room. Two men dressed in green scrubs were gathering equipment from cabinets. With everything in place, one of the men pulled on a latch to open a door. He reached in, rolled out a stretcher that obviously held a body covered with a white sheet, and wheeled it over next to the autopsy table. He removed the sheet, revealing the body of an obese woman. The other man helped lift her from the stretcher to the table.

Looking directly at us for the first time, he said, "My name is Dr. Bara. I am the medical examiner, and this is Dr. Elmsley, who will be assisting me today. What we have here is a middle-aged woman, Mrs. Theungen, who collapsed and died on a sidewalk downtown. She had no known medical problems. We are required by law to look for the cause of death."

Dr. Bara removed the hospital gown covering Mrs. Theungen, and Dr. Elmsley placed a towel over her pelvic area. I was impressed by the respect shown for the body of a deceased person.

Dr. Bara held a small recorder in his hand as he examined Mrs. Theungen's body and recorded his observations of her size, color, skin condition, and presence of any scars. After completing the visual inspection, which he stated was unremarkable, he made a long Y-shaped incision extending from her armpits to the pubic bone. It felt creepy, and yet I was captivated. Suddenly, the room was filled with a putrid, nauseating odor, making me feel queasy and more focused on how to breathe without taking in the horrific smell than on the autopsy itself.

No one was saying a word about the offensive odor, acting as if it didn't exist. The medical examiner opened the chest cavity to examine Mrs. Theungen's heart and lungs. He was describing what he was seeing, but I had lost interest. *What is that smell?* It was all I could think about.

Next he began to examine the abdominal cavity. He lifted her liver and showed us the location of the gallbladder.

"Ah, a ruptured gallbladder and a raging infection—the source of the odor. I suspect that caused her death."

I remembered the saying "fair, fat, and forty" to describe the typical profile of a person with gallbladder disease.

Using a scalpel, he removed her liver and held up the wedged-shaped, flabby, reddish-gray organ for us to see before placing it on the scales and recording its weight. It weighed three pounds and two ounces, an average size according to Dr. Bara. Next, he began slicing it into thin pieces.

I was watching intently when I heard someone ask, "Are you okay?"

It was then I noticed I was sweating profusely, and the sights were getting dimmer. Before I could answer, two people were holding me up and telling me to walk with them. They dragged me out of the morgue, and I heard what sounded like a faraway voice say, "Sit down."

I plopped down and landed on the lap of an outpatient waiting to be seen in the clinic. Someone giggled as my helpers lifted me off the patient and placed me on the bench.

Pushing on my back, one of my helpers said, "Put your head down between your legs."

I did as I was commanded and nearly toppled to the floor before they caught me. The sounds around me gradually got louder, and my sight returned.

Miss Slusser arrived and sent my helpers back to the morgue. She took me to the cafeteria and gave me a glass of water. We sat and chatted as I recovered, before she suggested I go back to the dormitory and rest. I went without protesting.

The following morning, one of my assigned patients was Mr. Householder, a thirty-seven-year-old currently in surgery for a cholecystectomy (gallbladder removal). I decided not to mention yesterday's incident but wait to see if Miss Slusser brought it up. She didn't.

Mr. Householder was due back on the unit before noon. I had time to take care of my other patient and prepare Mr. Householder's room for his arrival. It was my first time to set up Wangensteen suction to draw stomach contents through the nasogastric tube Mr. Householder would have in place.

Miss Slusser watched as I fiddled around with the glass bottles and tubing before asking for help. She was patient and guided me through the steps. It was simple once I understood the dynamics.

Mr. Householder arrived from the recovery room around noon. I helped the recovery room staff lift him to his bed, being careful not to dislodge his Foley catheter, nasogastric tube, intravenous line, and T-tube (catheter in the common bile duct). Once all the tubes were draining properly, I listened to the recovery room nurse's report and reviewed the doctor's orders.

Every half hour until two in the afternoon, and then hourly, I checked his vital signs, dressing, drainage tubes, and IV. He was to receive one hundred milliliters of IV solution every hour. Using a formula, I calculated the number of drips per minute needed to deliver the correct amount and adjusted the slide clamp on the tubing until it was dripping at the right rate. To ensure he was getting the right amount, I placed a piece of adhesive tape from the bottom of the bottle to the neck and marked the tape with times to show where the solution level should be each hour.

Before leaving for the day, I gave him pain medication and had him do coughing and deep breathing exercises. His coughs were wimpy.

"You need to cough harder to clear your lungs."

"I can't. It hurts."

I supported his abdomen with a pillow. "Take a deep breath and cough hard."

He tried. I kept telling him to try again until he finally coughed harder and brought up some mucus. If looks could kill, I would have been sprawled out on the floor.

The next morning, after I gave Mr. Householder a bed bath and a back rub, I helped him get out of bed to sit in a chair. His tall slim stature did not fit the typical profile of a person with gallbladder disease.

"How tall are you?" I asked.

"Six foot five."

"Wow, I feel like a grasshopper."

On the second postoperative day, I helped him ambulate in the room. I sat him on the edge of the bed and assisted his stepping down onto the footstool and to the floor. As he stood by the bed, I gathered the IV pole, urine drainage bag, and T-tube drainage bag in one hand and hooked my other arm around his arm. We began walking. Suddenly, his full body weight was leaned against my body. Mr. Householder had fainted. We fell to the floor with Mr. Householder landing on me. The loud crash brought staff running to the scene. Once they determined we were okay, I got up, and the staff who'd come to the room assisted Mr. Householder and all his tubes back to the bed. Amazingly, everything was intact. The only thing broken was my pride.

Following the incident, Miss Slusser took me to a private area. I knew I was about to be chastised. Looking me straight in the eye, she asked in an irritated tone, "Why didn't you get help?"

"He did well yesterday when I sat him in a chair. I thought I could walk him without assistance," I replied in a soft, meek voice.

"You had all that equipment to manage and were in no position to help if he got light-headed," she said, obviously still annoyed with me.

"You're right. I made a bad decision."

Her voice softened, and she said, "Tall patients are more prone to fainting."

"I didn't know that."

She explained, "Tall people get light-headed more easily when they stand up. Blood is pulled downward by gravity, leaving a decreased supply to the brain. It takes longer for a tall person's body to adjust. Dehydration, weakness, pain, medication, and vasovagal stimulation following gallbladder surgery are additional contributing factors that made Mr. Householder a prime candidate for fainting."

She impressed me with her knowledge. I hadn't considered all that before making my decision to walk Mr. Householder without help. The next time I got him up, I solicited help. He progressed well and was discharged twelve days later.

I wanted to make a good impression on Mr. Jarok, a good-looking sixteen-year-old with dark brown hair, brown eyes, and smooth skin, only three years younger than me. He had just returned from the recovery room following a spinal fusion and insertion of a Harrington rod for treatment of scoliosis. Dr. Jackson used bone fragments from Mr. Jarok's tibia and placed the stainless steel Harrington rod alongside his spine. A body cast was applied. It extended high on his neck and prevented him from turning his head.

As I arrived at his bedside, Mr. Jarok mumbled something.

Leaning close to his face and looking directly at him I said, "I'm sorry, I didn't hear what you said."

"I think I'm going to throw up." He promptly vomited, hitting me smack in the face.

I attempted to tilt Mr. Jarok on his side to keep him from aspirating, while turning my head to vomit on the floor. Once we stopped upchucking, I left the room to clean myself up. Fortunately, the vomitus did not get on my clothes. I found a towel, washcloth, and mouthwash and scrubbed my face vigorously before swishing the mouthwash around in my mouth for at least a full minute. When I regained my composure, I returned to his room, cleaned him, and gave him an injection of Phenergan for the nausea.

He apologized profusely.

"You couldn't help it. I shouldn't have put my face directly in front of you. Lesson learned."

Mr. Madden was only forty-four years old and had terminal pancreatic cancer. It was heartbreaking to see this young man, who only a year ago was an active, vibrant husband and father of two teenage boys, lying in bed with intractable pain.

I knew the morphine I was about to give him would provide very little pain relief. I felt Mr. Madden's arms, legs, and buttocks in search of a possible site. Everywhere I checked, his muscles were hard as a rock. I plunged the needle with twice the normal force, and it went into his thigh. I pushed the medicine slowly into the muscle. Using a cotton ball, I applied pressure to the site for a minute after removing the needle. Still, the morphine oozed back out.

Mrs. Scott, my other assigned patient, was an elderly female diagnosed with herpes zoster (shingles) of the eye. She was in isolation. I put on a mask, gown, and gloves before going into her room.

Her forehead and the skin surrounding her eye were bright red with blisters filled with water.

"This is the worst pain I've ever had, and I've had five children," she said. "It comes without warning, and it's horrific. When is this going to go away?"

"It usually takes a couple of weeks. Does the pain medicine help?"

"Not much. It makes me fall asleep, but only for a short time. The pain is still there when I wake up. I can't see out of my left eye. Will I get my sight back?"

"Has the eye doctor checked you?"

"He looked in my eye yesterday and ordered some eye drops. I asked him about my sight. He said it depended on the amount of scarring the infection caused, and wouldn't give me a yes or no answer. I hope I get it back. Oh, the pain is starting. I can't take this. Please help me."

She was in agony. I wanted to make her pain go away. "I'll check to see if it's time for more medicine."

I removed my gown and gloves, washed my hands, removed my mask, threw it in the wastebasket by the door, and went to the utility room to wash my hands again. It had recently been discovered that the same virus caused chicken pox and herpes zoster. I could not get chicken pox since I'd had the disease as a child, but I had been told I could spread the herpes zoster virus to others and cause them to get chicken pox if they'd never had chicken pox.

I prepared some morphine and returned to her room after gowning, gloving, and masking again. By the time I returned to the dorm, I was drained and wondered why there had to be so much suffering.

My father was scheduled for a bilateral inguinal hernia repair. He had not been in a hospital since 1931, at age nineteen, following an automobile accident. I immediately remembered his horror story.

Dad had a deep ugly scar that extended from the middle of his abdomen to the center of his back. As a small child, I had peeked at it and then quickly looked away. It was grotesque. When I was older, I'd asked him about the scar.

He told me, "My friend Jack and I went out one Saturday night. We had a few drinks, and Jack wrecked the car. It flipped over several times before landing upside down in a ditch. I lost consciousness and don't know how long it took someone to find us. Days later, I woke up confused and didn't know where I was. My head felt like it had been hit with a sledgehammer. Someone yelled, 'He's trying to get up. He's awake.'

"I was struggling to get up, but sharp pains shot through my stomach. A lady grabbed my arms and said, 'You need to lie down and be still.' I plopped down on the bed and asked where I was. 'You're in the hospital. You've been here ten days,' she said.

"When I asked what happened, she told me about the accident and said she was going to call my doctor and tell him I was awake.

"My doctor walked in the room with a big grin. His first words were, 'Welcome back. You're lucky to be alive.'

"I wasn't feeling very lucky. My head was throbbing and my stomach hurt. He flashed a light in my eyes and then started poking on my stomach and asking me to tell him where it hurt. I yelled in pain. It felt like he was stabbing me. He left, saying he would see me later that evening. I realized after he was gone I didn't know his name and asked the nurse.

"That evening when Dr. Madison returned, I had a high fever and my stomach was swollen and hard. He called in a surgeon. The surgeon, Dr. Lusk, scheduled me for exploratory surgery in the morning. He didn't know what the problem was.

"After surgery, Dr. Lusk told me my right kidney was crushed. He had to remove it. There was a bad infection where my kidney had been, and Dr. Lusk had to leave the wound open for it to drain and heal. What I didn't know, until later, was he didn't expect me to live."

It would be twelve years before the discovery of the first antibiotic, penicillin. My father remained in the hospital for an entire year. He said it was touch and go many times during that year before he finally turned the corner.

He and my mother had met one month before the accident. She visited him every day at the hospital. The day he was discharged, Dr. Lusk told him he would have to take it easy the rest of his life.

Laughing, my dad said, "We eloped the next day."

Now at age fifty-three, Dad was admitted to the hospital the day before his scheduled surgery. I visited him in the evening before surgery and asked him if he was scared.

"No," he replied, looking at me with a puzzled expression.

"I was thinking about the last time you were in the hospital and thought you might be scared."

"This should be a piece of cake," he said.

Before leaving, I hugged him and said, "I'll see you tomorrow afternoon."

He was sleeping when I walked into his room. Mom was sitting in a chair beside his bed. I wasn't prepared to see how pale he looked.

"How's he doing?" I asked.

"The doctor said everything went well. He's been sleeping since he came back."

We sat and chatted quietly.

Shortly after he was awake, Dad said, "Let me sit up in a chair."

"I guess you are feeling pretty good," I said, "but I'll have to check with the nurse. You may have to stay in bed until tomorrow morning."

"I want to sit in the chair and smoke a cigar," he demanded.

"I'll be right back. I'm going to find the nurse."

The nurse returned to his room with me and told him he would have to stay in bed for today. Dad was agitated but rested his head back on the pillow in resignation.

Two days later, Dad developed a paralytic ileus, a complete loss of motility of the intestines. The nurse inserted a nasogastric tube and connected it to Wangensteen suction to drain his stomach. I asked his surgeon what had caused the paralytic ileus.

"I had to handle his intestines during the hernia repair. That could cause it, but I don't know for sure. Most of my patients don't have this happen after a hernia repair."

I wondered if it was related to his previous hospital experience and suspected stress was a contributing factor. Several days later the surgeon detected bowel sounds, and from that point on his recovery progressed smoothly.

The hospital was building an addition, with some private patient rooms, as well as bathrooms with showers in all the patient rooms. I was thinking how luxurious that was going to be for the patients and the staff when I walked into the six-bed men's ward to meet my patient, Mr. Gehring, a teenager who had broken his femur.

"Good morning. My name is Miss Swan, and I'll be taking care of you today," I said.

"Why can't I have a pretty young student nurse?" one of the men in the ward shouted while the others laughed.

"Because I'm special," Mr. Gehring said with a broad smile on his face.

I was glad he had chimed in because I was embarrassed and didn't know what to say.

"You're stupid, not special," said a big burly man lying in the bed next to him.

"Yeah. Anyone who tries jumping from the hood of one moving car to another has a loose screw in his head," said another as everyone in the room joined in the heckling.

The guys were getting rowdy, so I said, "That's enough."

"Oh, listen to her. She's trying to act all professional," said one of the men, with a long drawl on the word *professional*.

Ignoring the comment, I focused on my patient.

Mr. Gehring's left leg had been placed in traction two days earlier, waiting for the swelling to go down before a cast could be applied. Today, he was scheduled for surgery. Dr. Strange planned to put him in a hip spica cast. It would cover Mr. Gehring's trunk and extend down his left leg to below his knee and to his midthigh on the right leg. I wanted to give Mr. Gehring a good refreshing bath before he went to surgery. It would be a long time before he could wash all over again. When I finished, I gave him his preoperative injection of Demerol and atropine.

Thirty minutes later, Dr. Strange stopped by Mr. Gehring's room for a final check on the swelling. "Everything looks good. I'll see you in surgery in about fifteen minutes."

I was gone for the day before Mr. Gehring returned to his room.

Plans were made for Mr. Gehring to stay in the hospital until his cast dried. After discharge, his mother would care for him. Arrangements were made for a public health nurse to visit him on the day of discharge and several times a week.

During morning report several days after his discharge, I learned Mr. Gehring was back in the hospital. He, or someone, had removed his big heavy cast.

The nurse said, "Dr. Strange was peeved, to put it mildly, and asked Mr. Gehring why he removed the cast. He said it was too hot and uncomfortable."

I was in the nursing station later that morning when Dr. Strange walked in scratching his groin and announced, "Mr. Gehring has pubic lice."

I began to itch. Dr. Strange ordered treatment and rescheduled surgery for reapplication of the cast.

Miss Fishman was emaciated. Her skin lay wrinkled over her sunken cheeks, and her red hair was matted to her head. I imagined she had once been a beautiful woman with long curly locks flowing down her back, full lips painted pink, and high cheekbones with just enough rouge to make them glow. I felt sad seeing her wasting away with a disease that could have been treated if diagnosed in its early stages.

She was receiving treatment for tertiary syphilis, late-stage syphilis. It could have been twenty years since her initial infection. Venereal diseases reached epidemic proportions in the United States after the World War II. Many servicemen returning home had syphilis or gonorrhea. Stateside, the US government waged a war against its spread. Educational songs and programs were placed in jukeboxes across the United States of America and could be played without inserting money. Film clips on venereal disease were shown in movie theaters before the main feature.

Treponema pallidum, the spirochete causing syphilis, can invade any organ but most often migrates to the bone, liver, stomach, heart, aorta, or central nervous system if untreated. Miss Fishman had central nervous system involvement, which was confirmed with a positive test result following a spinal tap. Here prognosis was poor.

Treatment included intravenous fluids, pain medication, and penicillin injections every eight hours. The damage couldn't be reversed, and there was no guarantee the treatment would prevent her condition from worsening.

Through the years, the spirochete had multiplied in Miss Fishman's body and attacked her spinal cord, causing degeneration of nerve fibers. She had trouble with balance and required assistance to walk. Standing with her feet wide apart to maintain balance, she lifted each foot high with every step and made loud slapping sounds when her feet hit the floor. She winced in pain as sharp bolts of pain shot down her spine and legs.

I gave her the penicillin and pain shot. A one-and-a-half-inch needle was too long for her wasted muscle tissue. I chose a one-inch needle. Miss Fishman yelled in pain when I plunged the short needle in and hit bone.

"I'm so sorry," I said and massaged the area gently for about a minute.

Later that week, Dr. Matthews wrote an order to discontinue her IV. After pulling the needle out, I walked down the hall pushing the IV pole and carrying the used equipment. A patient accidentally bumped into me, causing the used needle to stick into the palm of my hand. I felt a sting and saw a drop of blood ooze out of the wound. Instantaneously, I could hear Miss Brown's words reverberating in my head. "Tertiary syphilis cannot be transmitted by sexual contact. The only way to contract it is by getting some of the patient's blood in an open wound." I disposed the used equipment and hurriedly went in search of Miss Slusser.

"You won't believe what just happened. I got stuck with the needle I took out of Miss Fishman." I showed her my hand, which was still oozing blood.

"Oh no! Wash your hands and then go to the emergency room and get that puncture treated. I'll call and let them know I'm sending you," she said.

The ER nurse instructed me to scrub my hand with soap and water for five minutes. When I finished scrubbing, the doctor gave me a cream containing mercury to rub on the wound and handed me a prescription to get a blood test for syphilis immediately and once a month for four months.

I asked, "Why immediately?"

"We have to get a baseline to show you are negative for syphilis at this time."

I got the blood test, but not without explaining to the lab tech why I was getting it. I was embarrassed. One of the lab technicians teased me by smiling and saying, "Right. I've heard a lot of excuses. Usually it's the toilet seat."

Even though I didn't feel like smiling, I laughed and said, "I thought you would like to hear something different."

I was grateful each time the test results came back negative. On my last visit to the lab, I found the tech who had teased me and said, "You won't be seeing me again. I've decided to turn over a new leaf."

She laughed and said, "I knew it. I never believed your story."

Grace was fifteen years old and the only patient in a semiprivate room at the end of the hall on the medical surgical unit. The night nurse reported she was admitted to the unit in the night following an emergency appendectomy. That was it. No additional information was given about Grace. My curiosity was aroused. Too many details were missing. What was her last name? Who was her doctor? Was she on bed rest? Had she been given pain medicine?

I got busy working with my patients and forgot about it, until I saw a man and woman standing in the hall by Grace's room talking with an obstetrician. My curiosity was renewed, and I decided to investigate the matter. I told my instructor about the report and what I had seen.

She accompanied me to a private area and whispered, "I'm going to tell you something very confidential. Grace is a prominent family's daughter who delivered a baby last night. They brought her to the emergency room yesterday for severe abdominal pain and were told their daughter was in labor and about to deliver a baby. Grace has not been allowed to see her baby. Her parents are making arrangements to put it up for adoption."

When parents found out their daughter was pregnant, it was common for them to meet with the boy's parents to decide what to do. If marriage was not an option, the girl was sent to a home for unwed mothers during the later stages of pregnancy, and the family fabricated a story about where their daughter was during that time. The girl did not have any rights. She was either asked to sign or coerced into signing surrender papers before the baby was born.

I didn't know if Grace or the baby's father knew she was pregnant. If they knew, perhaps they'd considered getting an abortion. Since abortions were illegal, most abortions were self-induced or performed by a back alley butcher. It wasn't unusual to hear about a girl throwing herself down a flight of stairs, using a wire coat hanger or knitting needle, or ingesting a dangerous substance in an attempt to abort a fetus. Those who made arrangements to get an illegal abortion did not fare much better. The places were often filthy, and crude dirty instruments were used. Thousands of women died each year from botched abortions or infections.

I saw Grace the following morning when she was being discharged. A nurse was pushing her in a wheelchair with her parents walking silently behind them. Grace's eyes were downcast.

When I discovered my next assigned patient was Mrs. Morgan, I was concerned. I had known her from childhood. She recognized me immediately, even though we had not seen each other in five years and was eager to tell her story.

"I'm having surgery today. It's the strangest thing. Several months ago, I was in an automobile accident, and my chest slammed into the steering wheel. A bystander summoned an ambulance. Nothing was broken, but the doctor felt a lump in each breast. He said the lumps were hematomas caused by burst blood vessels, and they would go away over time. Well, they didn't go away. I called my family doctor. He took one look at me and sent me to a surgeon. That's when I started to get scared."

While she was talking the surgeon, Dr. Peterson, arrived and said, "I need to have you sign a consent for surgery. After we put you to sleep, I will take tissue from each lump and send it to the lab for a frozen biopsy. It won't take long to get the results. The pathologist will call me in the operating room with the findings, and I'll proceed from there. If the lumps are cancerous, I will remove your breasts, all the lymph nodes in the area, and the chest wall muscles. Do you have any questions?"

Mrs. Morgan gave a long sigh and asked, "Have you ever removed both breasts on someone?"

"Not at the same time," he said.

"How long will I be in surgery?"

"It depends on what I have to do. Do you have any more questions?" he asked as he placed the form on the bedside table for her to sign.

"I guess not," she said as she took the pen from his hand and signed the form.

"Good. I'll see you in the operating room in a few hours."

I helped Mrs. Morgan prepare for surgery. Thirty minutes after receiving a shot of Demerol and atropine, she was fast asleep, her husband and son sitting at her bedside. Two orderlies arrived with a stretcher at ten thirty. She woke up when they moved her and gave her husband and son a kiss before they wheeled her away.

Mrs. Morgan had not returned from surgery when I left the hospital for the day. I suspected she'd had to have her breasts removed.

That evening, I couldn't stop thinking about Mrs. Morgan. She had been my Sunday school teacher at a small country church near our home in Elyria, Ohio, when I was in the fifth and sixth grades. She and her family lived in a big brick house a couple of miles from our small cinder block home. There was a large pond and hill behind the house. During the winter when the pond was frozen, my brother, sister, and I would walk to their pond with our ice skates hanging over our shoulders and carrying our sleds. If Mr. Morgan knew we were on our way, he would build a fire in a large barrel. When our hands and feet got cold, we would thaw them out by the fire.

I was worried about the outcome of Mrs. Morgan's surgery. The survival rate for breast cancer patients was around 50 percent. I couldn't find any statistics in my books on the survival rate for patients who had cancer in both breasts. Naturally, I speculated her chances were slim.

Morning report confirmed my suspicions. Mrs. Morgan had had a double mastectomy. I was shocked when I walked into her room. She looked like she had aged ten years.

She smiled feebly when she saw me and said, "He had to remove both my breasts."

"I know. I was hoping the biopsies would be benign."

"Me too. I had a feeling this was going to happen. The first thing I did when I woke up was to feel my chest, and I knew. I wanted to see Ernest," she said, referring to her husband, and I began crying. The nurse must have heard me because she came over and patted me gently on my arm. When I asked to see him she said, 'He's waiting to see you. As soon as we move you back to your room, you can see him.'

"I told her I was ready and she said, 'It won't be too much longer. I'll call the anesthesiologist and ask him to check you. If he gives the green light, we will take you to your room.'

"That made me feel a little better. My husband was so sweet when I finally got to see him. He gave me a kiss and said he loved me. I started crying again, and he thought he had done something wrong. I told him he hadn't made me cry. It just felt so good to have him there with me."

I got a little teary-eyed and wasn't sure what to say. Everything seemed too trite, but in an effort to say something, I responded, "He's a good man."

I took care of her before leaving for the weekend and asked if I could take care of Mrs. Morgan when I returned. Miss Slusser denied my request, saying she wanted one of my classmates to have the experience of taking care of her. She said she would assign me to her care at a later time.

The day before I was assigned to take care of Mrs. Morgan again, the radiologist had brought a lead box containing radium tubes and, using tongs, placed them in Mrs. Morgan's uterus. They would be left in her for three days.

The head nurse gave me specific instructions, saying, "The total time you can be in Mrs. Morgan's room today is forty-five minutes. Keep track of your time. You will get too much radiation in one day if you stay longer. Don't stand at the foot of her bed. That is the direction where the most radiation is emitted from her body. Keep her door closed."

Gathering everything I needed, I peeked in her room and asked if there was anything she needed. She didn't have any requests, so I pushed the cart with the supplies through the doorway. A lead box was sitting on the floor. It would be used to transport the radiation tubes back to the lab and served as a constant reminder of the presence of radioactive material.

"Good morning, Mrs. Morgan," I said, putting fresh ice water in her bedside pitcher. "My time is limited to forty-five minutes in your room today. I'll have to work quickly to get everything done."

"The doctor told me I was radioactive, and the staff's time would be limited."

While bathing her, I asked if she had seen her chest when her doctor changed the dressings.

"No. He asked if I wanted to look, but I didn't want to. Maybe when it heals more, I'll look."

After finishing with her care, I said, "Call me if you need anything. I have ten minutes left."

On the third day, the radiologist arrived carrying a pair of gloves and an apron. "You need to leave the room. As soon as I take the tubes out, she won't be radioactive."

That day was the last time I saw Mrs. Morgan. Years later, my sister informed me Mrs. Morgan survived another thirty-five years. She had seen her sitting on a bench in a department store, and Mrs. Morgan had told her the cancer had returned.

My sister said, "She looked thin and weak. I knew she didn't have much longer. Mrs. Morgan told me she'd had a good life and never thought she would live to the age of eighty-two. A week later, I saw her name in the obituaries."

It was my last day on the unit. Next week, I would be in obstetrics, my first specialty rotation.

OBSTETRICAL NURSING

I hopped out of bed at five thirty to get ready for my new assignment. It was one of only a handful of mornings I hopped out of bed and sprinted into action when the alarm sounded. In record time, I showered, dressed, and arrived in the cafeteria early to join my classmates. They were surprised to see me.

Nancy Jezewski asked laughingly, "Are you sick?"

"No, just out of my mind. I can't wait to get to labor and delivery. Sorry I'm ruining your dreams of becoming a millionaire," I said, remembering the day she told me she would be a millionaire if she had a penny for every day I threatened to quit because I had to get up so early.

After breakfast, I walked up to the double doors labeled "Labor and Delivery: Authorized Personnel Only." I paused to savor the moment before entering. Expecting to hear women screaming, I felt relieved to hear only the sound of Mrs. Schroeder, my instructor, saying, "Good morning."

Mrs. Schroeder was a petite middle-aged woman who surprised me by sporting a big smile and looking genuinely glad to see me. I had seen her a year and a half earlier at our welcoming reception, a few times in the cafeteria, and two days in the classroom, but had never had a conversation with her.

She escorted me to a locker room, where there was a rack of green scrubs and said, "After you change your clothes and wash your hands, I'll give you your assignment."

As I was changing into scrubs, I thought about *The Cry and the Covenant*, a book written by Dr. Ignaz Semmelweis advocating hand washing using an antiseptic solution before examining patients and delivering babies. Dr. Semmelweis lived in the early 1800s. Women delivering babies in hospitals were dying within days, while those giving birth at home were surviving. Doctors went from autopsies to delivering babies without washing their hands. They wiped their bloody hands on their lab coats and proudly wore the bloody coats as a badge of honor. The physicians clung to their beliefs, refusing to wash and disinfect their hands.

Wearing scrubs for the first time made me feel big league. I washed my hands, put on some scrubs, and found Mrs. Schroeder.

"It's quiet back here this morning. We only have two patients. Both are in early labor. Of course, things can change rapidly. I'll have you stay with Mrs. Wysocki. She is twenty-two years old, and this is her first pregnancy. You can time her contractions, monitor the fetal heart rate, and keep her comfortable."

Mrs. Wysocki was lying on her back in a private labor room. Her belly looked mountainous. We chatted briefly before Mrs. Schroeder placed my hand on her abdomen and told me to use my fingertips to feel the contractions.

"You'll feel the uterine muscles start to tighten. Write down the time you feel the beginning of a contraction and the time it ends. Keep your hand on her belly between contractions and note each time one starts and ends. That will provide a record of the frequency and length of her contractions."

I kept my fingertips in place and was able to time a contraction. When it ended, Mrs. Schroeder counted the baby's heart rate and handed the stethoscope to me. She didn't tell me her count, but had me count for a full minute. "It's 144," I said.

"I counted 140, so you're right on the money," she said.

Mrs. Wysocki asked, "Is that normal?"

"Yes," Mrs. Schroeder answered. "The baby's heart rate normally is somewhere between 120 and 160 beats a minute."

"Move the stethoscope over her abdomen and tell me what you hear."

"I hear a slower heartbeat."

"That's Mrs. Wysocki's heart rate. Be careful when checking the baby's heart rate that you aren't counting Mom's heartbeat."

Mrs. Wysocki grinned from ear to ear when Mrs. Schroeder called her Mom.

"Check Mrs. Wysocki's vital signs and the baby's heart rate every hour and keep a record of the contractions. I'll be back in about an hour. Ring the call bell if you need me sooner."

After my instructor left, Mrs. Wysocki looked at me intently with what I thought was fear in her eyes. I wondered if she were afraid of having an inexperienced student nurse at her bedside.

As quickly as I had that thought, she said, "I'm glad you're here with me."

My confidence was boosted immediately, and I realized it didn't matter what I knew. Having someone in the room with her was what really mattered. Only the hospital staff was permitted in the labor and delivery area due to the fear of germs.

In the waiting room, fathers-to-be could be seen pacing about as they anxiously awaited the news of their babies' births. After a baby was born, the doctor would go to the waiting room to tell the father he had a baby boy or girl. The next time the proud new father came to the hospital, he would have a few cigars sticking out of his shirt pocket. The cigars would have either a blue or a pink band around them, with the words, "It's a boy," or, "It's a girl." The cigars were given to family members, friends, strangers, and to me, occasionally, to announce the baby's birth.

I pulled up a chair, sat down, and put my hand on Mrs. Wysocki's belly. Her contractions were five minutes apart and lasted thirty seconds. We talked between her contractions. Like most expectant mothers, she'd suspected she was pregnant when she missed a period and had made an appointment to see Dr. Hennings, a local obstetrician. He'd asked if she wanted to have a pregnancy test.

The Friedman test consisted of injecting some of the woman's urine into a rabbit's vein. Forty-eight hours later, the rabbit's ovaries were examined. The pregnancy test was positive if large bumps were present on the ovaries. Instead of telling the woman the test was positive, the euphemism "the rabbit died" was used. All rabbits died because they were killed to examine the ovaries. Most people were not aware of this, but everyone knew that "the rabbit died" meant the woman was pregnant.

Mrs. Wysocki did not want a pregnancy test. Dr. Hennings confirmed her pregnancy by examination.

Mrs. Wysocki said, "It seems like I've been waiting forever to find out if we're having a boy or girl. We've had fun trying to guess. At my baby shower, my friends put my wedding band on a string and dangled it over my belly. It swung back and forth. They said that meant I was having a girl. If it had swung in circles, I was carrying a boy. They asked if I had morning sickness and craved sweets or salt. When I told them I had morning sickness and coveted sweets, they were sure I was having a girl. My belly looked like there was a watermelon inside, which confirmed their prediction. A basketball shape would have meant a boy. They convinced me. I think it's a girl."

"That does sound convincing. We'll see. These myths are about 50 percent accurate. I hope you didn't decorate your nursery for a girl."

"I didn't. I thought about it, but my husband wasn't so sure."

As Mrs. Wysocki's contractions grew stronger, longer, and more frequent, she groaned with each one and rested between them. Before leaving for lunch, I massaged her lower back and gave her ice chips, the only thing she was allowed to have since having been admitted.

When I returned, I was struck by the change in Mrs. Wysocki's appearance from when we'd first met. Her hair was tangled, her facial muscles were taut, and she looked exhausted.

An RN had checked Mrs. Wysocki while I was at lunch. Her cervix was dilated to seven centimeters. I was excited to think that I would see my first delivery today.

At three thirty in the afternoon, Mrs. Wysocki had not dilated the three additional centimeters to reach full dilation. It was time to leave. I was disappointed. After being with Mrs. Wysocki all day, I would miss out on the culminating moment. I told her goodbye, and she managed to smile.

The next morning, before going to labor and delivery, I stopped by the nursery window to take a peek. There I spotted a bassinet with a blue name tag labeled "Wysocki boy" with the cutest tiny baby sleeping peacefully.

I found Mrs. Wysocki and said, "I just saw your beautiful baby boy. Congratulations."

Beaming with joy, she said, "Thanks. He's the most beautiful baby I've ever seen."

Mrs. Schroeder greeted me, saying, "It's going to be a busy day. There are five women in labor. I've assigned you to Mrs. Bennett in room 3. The nurse gave her Demerol and scopolamine about forty-five minutes ago. She's been screaming and trying to get out of bed. They had to put wrist restraints on her, and someone needs to stay with her at all times."

Scopolamine was used in obstetrics to produce twilight sleep and amnesia. It depresses the central nervous system, producing drowsiness; euphoria; and, in some cases, delirium.

Mrs. Bennett had her legs slung up on the side rail and was struggling to get out of bed. She saw me and yelled, "Get these things off me!"

"I'll help you get more comfortable," I said as I lifted her legs and put them back on the bed and adjusted her gown to cover her body. "My name is Miss Swan. I'm a student nurse, and I'm going to stay with you. You'll feel better if you try to lie still."

She was flushed and sweating, so I said, "You look hot. Let me wash your face. There are some washcloths and towels in the cabinet. I don't have to leave to get them." I took a few steps away from her to find a washcloth.

She started yelling, and I reassured her by saying, "I'm not leaving. Keep your eyes on me."

I was able to find what I needed, including a clean top sheet. Her sheet was crumpled and lying on the floor.

After I washed her face and put a sheet over her, I held her hand as I reached through the side rail and placed my other hand on her abdomen. "I'm going to time your contractions."

With the next contraction, she began screaming, writhing about, and pulling her wrists as hard as she could in an effort to get her hands free. My hand flew off her belly. She calmed down when the contraction ended.

"I can't check you when you flail about. I have to monitor how you and your baby are doing. Is there anything I can do to help you get more comfortable?" I asked.

"Take these things off!" she screamed, pulling on the restraints.

"I'll take them off if you promise to be still. If you can't do that, I'll have to put them back on," I explained.

"I promise."

I was nervous taking the restraints off but decided it was worth a try. She stayed true to her word and lay still, although she screamed, while I checked the fetal heart rate, took her vital signs, and timed her next contraction.

Mrs. Bennett's behavior changed. She talked and giggled incessantly. I had difficulty following what she was saying but managed to figure out she was telling me the milkman was the baby's father, and she didn't want her husband to find out. I decided she was talking under the influence of drugs and didn't believe her.

An hour and a half later, she began making grunting sounds with her contraction. I lifted the sheet and was relieved not to see a baby.

The nurse, Mrs. Smith, walked in and said, "Sounds like she's starting to push." After checking her, she said, "It won't be too long until we have a baby. Call me when you see the top of the baby's head."

My heart began racing. I was scared to be alone with Mrs. Bennett in this situation. Ten minutes later, the top of the baby's head appeared. I hollered for the nurse.

Mrs. Smith took one look and said, "She isn't ready. Wait until you can see the whole top of the head."

Mrs. Bennett pushed with each contraction as I watched vigilantly, thinking the baby was going to pop out. Another ten minutes passed before I could see more of the head and summoned Mrs. Smith again.

Finally, Mrs. Bennett was ready to be transported to the delivery room. I felt like shouting hallelujah.

Mrs. Smith said, "I'll call her doctor and get a stretcher."

I warned Mrs. Bennett, "Were going to move you to the delivery room." She started to get up. "No, don't get up. The nurse is getting a stretcher."

She lay back on the bed. Mrs. Smith returned with the stretcher and another nurse and handed me a scrub cap and mask. They got her on the stretcher, rolled her to the delivery room, helped to place her on a narrow table, and strapped her arms down by her side.

The tempo accelerated, and I was trying to take it all in. An anesthesiologist arrived and started an IV. The nurses put flannel stockings on the patient to keep her warm and lifted both her legs simultaneously up high into shiny metal stirrups. Mrs. Smith scrubbed Mrs. Bennett's perineum and inner thighs with an antiseptic solution.

Dr. Hennings popped his head in the doorway and said, "I'm here. How's she doing?"

"The baby's crowning," Mrs. Smith responded calmly.

"Okay. I'll get scrubbed."

He returned in a few minutes, spoke to Mrs. Bennett, and then sat down on a stool that was placed between the patient's legs. After donning sterile gloves, he placed sterile drapes over her thighs and lower abdomen, and told Mrs. Bennett to push with her next contraction. He watched as she pushed. "She's ready to have this baby. Go ahead and start the nitrous oxide."

Once Mrs. Bennett was asleep, Dr. Hennings picked up a pair of scissors and cut the perineum (an episiotomy) to make more room for the baby's head.

After completing the episiotomy, he told the nurse to push on Mrs. Bennett's abdomen with the next contraction. The nurse pushed, using both hands, and Dr. Hennings slipped forceps, which looked like tongs, along each side of the baby's head and began pulling the head out. He paused briefly and slipped a finger in to feel around the baby's neck. He told me he was making sure the cord wasn't wrapped around it. He resumed pulling, and the head emerged facedown. The baby turned on its own, and a shoulder appeared. After the shoulders were delivered, the rest of the baby slipped out quickly.

It was a boy. He was limp, blue, and coated with a white creamy material called vernix. For my benefit, Dr. Hennings said the baby was fine. He cleared mucus from the baby's nostrils and mouth with a bulb syringe and wiped his face with a sterile towel. The baby began to cry. I sighed a breath of relief.

Dr. Hennings cut the umbilical cord and handed the baby to the nurse. She took him to a table set up on one side of the delivery room. I stayed with the mother, as instructed, and watched the delivery of the placenta and the suturing of the episiotomy. By the time Dr. Hennings finished, the nurse had taken the baby to the nursery and was back in the delivery room.

Anesthesia was stopped, vital signs checked, and I helped transport Mrs. Bennett to the recovery area. She could see her baby for the first time after she was alert and moved to a room on the postpartum floor.

I followed Mrs. Smith back to the delivery room. It was a mess.

Surgical drapes, bloody towels, and sheets were lying on the floor. The nurse gathered all the equipment from the tables, and housekeeping staff picked up everything that had been thrown about. Then they stripped and scrubbed the delivery table, wiped down all the tables, mopped the floor, and had the room ready for the next delivery within a matter of minutes.

I was with my assigned patient when the nurse asked me to help with a new admission. Mrs. Struck was in her mid-thirties and pregnant with her eighth child. I was instructed to give Mrs. Struck a "3H" enema (high, hot, and a hell of a lot) and shave her. Mrs. Struck had attempted to shave her perineal area prior to her arrival. Pieces of cotton were stuck on areas where she had nicked the skin.

After completing the enema, I cleaned and reshaved her perineum to remove all the cotton, hairs, and stubble. I had just finished when Mrs. Struck looked at me and calmly announced, "The baby's coming."

In the classroom, Mrs. Schroeder told us to listen to our patients. I listened, believed, and shouted, "The baby's coming!"

Staff stormed into the room. The top of the baby's head was visible. They quickly got her to the delivery room table, handed me a large pad, and told me to push against the baby's head.

The nurse looked at me and said, "Hold the baby back until the doctor gets here." Then she looked at Mrs. Struck and said, "Don't push. Pant when you have a contraction. Your doctor is on his way."

She left me alone with the patient. I had the pad up against the baby's head. Mrs. Struck began having a contraction, and I told her to pant. I began panting to demonstrate how to do it correctly. While I panted, she pushed.

I was hesitant to push on the baby's head. My brother Kevin was born prematurely in 1941. According to my mother, her doctor strapped her legs together to prevent his birth. Twenty-four hours later, he removed the straps, and Kevin was born. He survived but was later diagnosed with cerebral palsy. I believed the cerebral palsy was caused by their attempt to prevent his early birth.

I could feel the baby moving out. I dropped the pad, caught the baby, and yelled, "The baby's here."

Mrs. Struck raised her head to see her baby girl, who was squealing. After capturing a glimpse, she fell back on the table and began to cry.

The nurse's first words to me as she entered the room were "Why didn't you hold it back?" I could see anger in her eyes.

"I couldn't" was all I said.

The nurse took the baby from my hands. I was in a fog. I could hear and see the staff but couldn't process what was happening. I was worried about getting kicked out of nursing school.

Mrs. Schroeder arrived, took me to another area, and asked, "What happened?"

I did my best at explaining the details and felt greatly relieved when she said, "You did the right thing."

Most of the male babies were brought back to the delivery room for a circumcision when they were one or two days old. The nurse, carrying a cute little baby asleep in her arms, and the obstetrician, Dr. Bassett, walked into the room.

The nurse placed him on a special board shaped like a baby, stretched out his arms and legs, and immobilized him by strapping his arms and legs to the board. The baby woke up and whimpered.

Dr. Bassett stepped in and, without using any anesthetic, freed the foreskin from the head of the penis using hemostats. The baby began crying louder. Next, Dr. Bassett placed a bell-shaped instrument over the head of the penis and stretched the foreskin over the bell. The baby was shrieking. When the doctor used a knife to free the foreskin, the baby got quiet momentarily, and then came ghostly shrills between gasps for air. Once the circumcision was completed, the nurse applied an adrenaline solution to stop the bleeding and placed Vaseline gauze over the wound.

Dr. Bassett said, "That went well."

That went well? I thought. *That was inhumane!*

Later, I spoke with Mrs. Schroeder about my feelings.

She explained, "Babies don't feel pain like older children and adults. Their nervous system isn't fully developed."

I didn't believe it. He wasn't shrieking and gasping for air for no reason.

Couldn't others in the room see and hear the baby? Would the day come when I became oblivious to the cries?

Every morning for the past month, before going to labor and delivery, I paused to peek though the nursery window at the tiny bundles of joy swaddled in their blankets. Today, two of my classmates and I walked into the nursery to begin our rotation. I was eager and ready to get started. Unfortunately, my most vivid memory of orientation to the nursery was being chided by Mrs. Schroeder. She showed us two canisters of cotton balls, one labeled clean and the other sterile, and instructed us to use forceps when removing a sterile cotton ball from the canister. At least that is what I heard.

Turning to me she said, "Give me a clean cotton ball."

I removed the lid on the container labeled clean and plucked out a cotton ball with my bare hand.

Mrs. Schroeder put her hands on her hips and with a raised voice said, "You just contaminated all the cotton balls. I can't believe you did that! Throw them in the trash."

Several nursery staff turned to look. My face suddenly grew hot, and I knew I had turned bright red as everyone gawked at me. After procuring another jar of clean cotton balls, she asked a classmate to get a cotton ball. My classmate removed one using the forceps. I didn't get it. What was the purpose of having clean and sterile if the same forceps were used to remove them? I was feeling too stupid and embarrassed to ask.

When Mrs. Schroeder finished showing us around, we students spent the remainder of the day watching and helping the nurses. I was scheduled to work a week in the regular nursery before being assigned to the special care nursery.

Before I left for the day, Mrs. James, the RN I had been observing said, "Take good care of your hands. We wash our hands at least thirty times a day."

I scrubbed my hands before taking care of two-day-old baby boy Farley. He was sleeping propped on his side with a blanket. I stood admiring his sucking movements and smiling. Before waking him, I counted his respirations and checked his heart rate.

When I checked his temperature, he wailed. I patted his back and spoke softly, to no avail. He continued to sob as I measured his head circumference and felt his anterior and posterior fontanels (soft spots on his head where his skull bones had not yet fused together). I counted his fingers and toes, bathed and weighed him, pinned on a clean diaper using diaper pins with blue heads, pulled his tiny arms through the sleeves of a white shirt, and wrapped him in a blanket.

After warming a bottle of formula, I picked him up and sat in a rocking chair. He sucked zealously and latched onto the nipple with all his might when I pulled it from his mouth to burp him.

The bawling began again. I held him over my shoulder and patted his back. He cried and cried but finally burped. I put the nipple back in his mouth.

Once again he was content, and he fell asleep before finishing his formula.

At ten in the morning, I carried him to his mother's room for a thirty-minute visit.

"Good morning, Mrs. Farley. I have someone I think you've been waiting to see. Let me check your wristband and see if it matches his. Yep, they match."

"I knew that was my baby. He looks just like his daddy," she said, reaching to take him from my arms. "How much did he weigh this morning? Did he drink his formula? How long has he been sleeping?" She asked each question without pausing for an answer.

"He weighed seven pounds and five ounces."

"He lost two ounces. Is there something wrong?"

"No, it's normal to lose a few ounces. He should start gaining weight by tomorrow."

She kissed his cheek and rocked him in her arms. He continued to sleep peacefully. She said, "I wish he would wake up."

"Have you decided on a name?"

"We named him Charles Andrew Farley Junior."

"Are you going to call him Charles?"

"I think we'll call him Charlie."

"I like that."

I left him with his mom and went back to the nursery to finish my charting.

Thirty minutes later, I returned to take Charlie back to the nursery.

Mrs. Farley asked, "Do you have to take him?"

"Yes," I told her. "I'll bring him back after lunch."

The babies were taken to their mothers three times a day. Fathers were not allowed in the room when the baby was there. They gazed at their babies through the nursery window during visiting hours each afternoon and evening. Newborns stayed in the hospital for about a week. Dads finally got to hold their babies for the first time upon discharge.

After a week in the regular nursery, I was moved to the nursery for babies with special needs. Baby Kellogg, Mrs. Kellogg's second child, had Rh-positive blood, and Mom's blood was Rh negative. He was a precious little boy who looked so normal, with perfect long slender fingers and toes, a round face, and curly dark hair, yet there was a war going on in his little body.

The Rh factor had not presented a problem with Mrs. Kellogg's first baby because her blood had never had contact with Rh-positive blood. Blood does not travel through the placenta from mother to baby, but antibodies do. During the birth of her first child, her blood came in contact with her baby's Rh-positive blood, and her body began to produce antibodies against the Rh factor. They were harmless until she became pregnant with her second child. The antibodies traveled through her placenta into baby Kellogg's blood and began destroying his red blood cells.

At birth, it was evident Baby Kellogg's red blood cells were being destroyed. He was anemic, and the whites of his eyes and his skin were slightly yellow. Bilirubin, a brownish-yellow substance, is a waste product of broken-down red blood cells. If the destruction of the blood cells is too rapid for the liver to manage, the bilirubin travels to other organs of the body, causing jaundice, brain damage, heart failure, and death. The pediatrician ordered frequent blood studies to test the newborn's bilirubin level. Baby Kellogg's heels looked like blue pincushions.

Phototherapy was ordered. I put gauze patches over his eyes to protect them from the ultraviolet rays, removed his shirt and diaper, and placed him under a fluorescent light. The light rays helped to break down the bilirubin for elimination from Baby Kellogg's body.

During visiting hours, I opened the curtains so his parents could see him. Baby Kellogg lay naked in his bassinet with his eyes covered. Mom and Dad peered through the window, and tears rolled down Mom's cheeks. Dad put his arm around Mom and pulled her close to him.

Slowly, Baby Kellogg's bilirubin level began to come down. He became more active, and his shrill weak cry became more robust. Mom was discharged from the hospital seven days after his birth. Baby Kellogg was discharged a week later. He was fortunate because, at the same time, another baby with Rh incompatibility was in the nursery. That one died when he was three days old.

Baby Turner weighed two pounds and twelve ounces at birth. I was in the nursery the morning he was rolled in in an incubator, with another nurse wheeling an oxygen tank alongside. Taking one look at his tiny body made me wonder if he had a chance of surviving. When time permitted, I asked the nurse about his prognosis.

She said, "The main thing is to keep him warm, keep his oxygen level up and airway clear, feed him, and keep him from getting an infection. If we can do that, he should make it."

I hadn't heard of many babies surviving who were that small, but I decided he did have a chance. My brother Kevin had survived at three pounds, and I'd survived being born at home and weighing an estimated four pounds.

I was assigned to take care of Baby Turner when he was ten days old. His weight was up to two pounds and fourteen ounces. He continued to need extra oxygen since his respiratory system was not fully developed. The oxygen was mixed with the air in the incubator to increase normal air oxygen concentration from 21 percent to 40 percent. Oxygen concentration levels in the incubator were checked every few hours to ensure the level did not exceed 40 percent. It had recently been discovered that higher oxygen levels could cause blindness in newborns. I was personally cognizant of this, since my brother Kevin had retinopathy from exposure to high oxygen levels in his incubator. He wasn't blind but had extremely poor eyesight.

Using a special soft preemie nipple made it easier for Baby Turner to suck. Reaching through the portholes of the incubator and holding his tiny head in the palm of one hand, I gave him his bottle. He worked hard to suck but didn't have the strength to get enough formula. His feedings were supplemented with extra fluid administered by hypodermoclysis. With steady hands and my stomach flip-flopping, I inserted two small needles under the skin on his back, one on each side near his shoulder blade, and taped them in place. Every three hours, I filled a syringe with half-strength normal saline and slowly pushed fifteen milliliters of fluid through each needle as I watched his skin balloon to the size of a golf ball on each side. Gradually, the fluid absorbed into his tissues, and the golf balls disappeared.

Using this method to give Baby Turner additional fluid was safer than giving it intravenously. There was only one size of tubing available for intravenous fluid administration, and the drops were too big for a tiny baby. It was difficult to control the flow rate using the slide clamp on the tubing, and giving too much fluid directly into his vein could result in heart failure.

I took care of Baby Turner for three days. My hands were getting red and chapped. I used hand lotion liberally and applied A&D ointment several times each evening after work. I didn't want them to crack and bleed, an ideal place for bacteria to hide. They stayed red and sore but never cracked. By the end of the week, Baby Turner weighed three pounds. That was my last day in the nursery. I would be rotating to the postpartum floor with the new mothers.

The women on postpartum looked amazingly different from those in labor and delivery. A rejuvenating glow and softness replaced the tense and tired facial expressions of labor. Mrs. Cahill had given birth to her third child, a little girl, nearly thirty-two hours before I met her. She lay in bed waiting for breakfast and morning care. I assisted her with her bath and gave her a long, relaxing back rub.

Since Mrs. Cahill was like the 90 percent of new mothers who chose not to breastfeed, she received a Delestrogen injection after delivery to help suppress the production of breast milk. I wrapped an unbleached muslin binder around her chest to keep her breasts from becoming engorged and pulled it as tight as I could before securing it with sixteen safety pins.

Mrs. Cahill was ready to get out of bed. Pulling the footstool up to her bedside, I assisted her as she stepped on the stool and then to the floor. Gingerly, she walked around in her room before sitting in a chair while I changed her bed sheets.

She complained of pain from the episiotomy. Once she was back to bed, I found a perineal lamp with a twenty-five-watt bulb and placed it about twelve inches from her perineum and helped prop her legs up. The heat from the light bulb was soothing and healing. Twenty minutes later, I returned to her room to remove the lamp. Mrs. Cahill was sound asleep.

She stirred about slightly as I removed the equipment, straightened her legs, and pulled the sheet and bedspread up over her.

Later that day, near the end of the shift, I was walking by the elevator and heard the bell sound. The door opened, and my sister Janet was in a wheelchair with her husband, Jerry, standing beside her. When the nurse wheeled her out of the elevator, Janet grabbed my arm and said, "Tell them I changed my mind. I want something for pain."

Janet had been planning on having her second child using the Lamaze method, which had been gaining popularity. She wanted to be alert when her baby was born, and for the past two months, she had attended Lamaze classes to learn breathing, relaxation, and visualization techniques to use during labor and delivery. These skills were designed to make the experience more comfortable without the use of medication.

Her labor pains were intense by the time she arrived at the hospital, and now Janet had a death grip on my arm. I walked beside her to the labor area and found a labor room nurse. After explaining the situation, I left her with the nurse and returned to the postpartum unit to see Jerry in the waiting room.

Janet's daughter, Carol, was born three hours after her arrival.

The next morning, she told me "I don't remember anything about her birth. They knocked me out."

The last patient I took care of before rotating to pediatrics was Mrs. Sutton, pregnant with her first child and admitted for treatment of preeclampsia. Her baby wasn't due for another month. During her routine checkup, her blood pressure was elevated, there was albumin in her urine, and she had gained seven pounds in two weeks. Her obstetrician decided to admit her for treatment.

Mrs. Sutton was alarmed. She told me, "I was doing well and felt really good. I had no idea anything was wrong when I went to my doctor. It's still hard to believe. I pray my baby will be okay."

"You were diagnosed in the early stages. Your doctor wanted you in the hospital where he could treat you and monitor you closely. How are you feeling this morning?"

"I feel okay. It's uncomfortable staying in bed all the time. I hate using the bedpan."

"Yeah, that has to be hard, especially when you feel good. Have you had any headaches or blurred vision?"

"No. What was my blood pressure this morning?"

"140 over 92."

"Whew, that's high. I usually am 110 over 70."

"Well the good news is it hasn't gone any higher than it was at the doctor's office. We're going to keep you sedated, give you a low-salt diet, and check your blood pressure every four hours."

"What will happen if my blood pressure gets higher?"

"There are some drugs the doctor can give you."

"Are they safe for my baby?"

"Yes," I told her.

Mrs. Sutton rested most of the day. There were no changes in her blood pressure and no new symptoms. The next morning when I went to her room and woke her, I noticed her eyelids were swollen. I checked her blood pressure, and it was 150/96.

I asked her how she was feeling, and she said, "I have a headache. Am I okay?"

"I'm going to let your doctor know. He can come in and check you and order some medicine," I said, hoping that would appease her.

Her obstetrician, Dr. Trollinger, was already at the hospital and came to check her immediately. After examining her and checking her urine for albumin he decided to induce labor and had her moved to the labor room.

I helped get her on the stretcher, gave her a hug, and said, "I'll see you tomorrow."

"And my baby?" she asked, looking straight into my eyes.

"And your baby," I said.

Mrs. Sutton delivered a healthy baby girl at four in the morning. She was back in her room by the time I arrived the next morning.

"Hi. It's good to see you. I hear you have a four-pound, thirteen-ounce girl. Have you seen her?"

"Not yet. My husband got to look at her through the nursery window. They had her in an incubator. The doctor told him she was breathing normally on her own, and they would keep her in the special care nursery to keep a close watch on her. He said she was bald. I can't wait to see her."

"Maybe they'll let me take you to the nursery window in a wheelchair so you can see her before I leave today."

"Please beg them. I want to see her."

"I'll do my best."

I massaged her fundus (the top of the uterus that can be felt through the abdominal wall) until it felt firm as a rock and checked her for bleeding. Everything looked normal. Her blood pressure was down to 128/80. It would take a few days before it was back to normal. There was still a slight danger of her having a convulsion, so the doctor had left orders to give her phenobarbital four times a day. Her eyes were still puffy, but her headache was gone.

Dr. Trollinger came around noon. I followed him to Mrs. Sutton's room and watched as he examined her. Since she didn't speak up, I asked, "Can I take her to see her baby this afternoon?"

"Not today. She should be able to see her tomorrow." He looked at Mrs. Sutton and said, "I saw her just before I came in here. She's doing well."

Mrs. Sutton was disappointed, but I proposed, "We have something to look forward to tomorrow."

The next morning after I gave Mrs. Sutton her morning care, I took her in a wheelchair to see her baby. A nurse wheeled the incubator up to the window, and Mrs. Sutton sat admiring her for at least five minutes.

Later that day, when it was time for me to leave, I stopped by to say goodbye to Mrs. Sutton. She thanked me for what I had done for her, and I thanked her for the privilege of being her student nurse and getting to know her.

PEDIATRIC NURSING

In spring 1963, I started my pediatric rotation. The most popular toys were the Easy-Bake Oven, the Mouse Trap board game, and the Tammy doll. A hospital stay cost twenty-eight dollars a day.

Miss Carpenter, my instructor, had a reputation of being tough. Older classmates forewarned us, saying, "She will drill you on every detail about your patients."

I was determined to not be daunted by my classmates' comments and decided Miss Carpenter expected us to learn and do our best. I hoped my best was good enough.

Miss Carpenter had looked friendly, not tough on the few occasions I had seen her. She and Mrs. Schroeder often came to the cafeteria together talking and smiling. I recalled one particular morning when

Miss Carpenter showed up with a gray cross smeared on her forehead. I thought it looked peculiar.

Clare, one of my Catholic classmates, said, "The priest put the sign of the cross on her forehead this morning during Ash Wednesday Mass. It's a sign of repentance."

"It looks funny. Why didn't she wash it off?" I asked.

"I don't know," she said.

I thought about it, and even though it made her face look dirty and she looked weird, I decided it was important enough for her to put all that aside and wear the cross. I respected her for that.

The first thing I heard upon entering the pediatric unit was a child screaming for Mommy. My heart melted. Yielding to my better judgment, I reluctantly followed my classmates into the nursing station instead of following my instinct to find and cuddle the child. The unit was dark and drab with no natural sunlight. It wasn't an inviting place for children. I thought about expectant parents preparing a nursery for their baby's arrival. When completed, it would be a cheery, bright, and welcoming place, not like the drab and dreary pediatric unit that emanated sickness and sadness.

Miss Carpenter was waiting for us. After the usual introductions, she handed each of us a paper with a long list of things to find and sent us on a scavenger hunt. I scurried around the unit finding everything on the list and took advantage of the remainder of the morning to look through charts, paying particular attention to the physicians' orders and medication dosages.

Miss Carpenter gave me my assignment for the next day. She had checked the surgery schedule and chose Dwight, who was scheduled to have a tonsillectomy and adenoidectomy (T&A) at ten o'clock the following morning. My classmates received their assignments and were able to look through their charts and meet their patients. I was moping. I didn't even know Dwight's age and felt cheated. Dwight would be admitted later in the day after I was gone. I asked to look through a chart of a patient who'd had a T&A. There weren't any. I was stuck gathering textbook information and left for the day feeling bummed out.

By the next morning, my mood had improved. Dwight was six years old and had a history of repeated bouts of tonsillitis. He was one of five children admitted the previous evening for a T&A. His lab work was done, and the surgeon and anesthesiologist had checked in on him soon after his admission.

Before going to Dwight's room, I reviewed his chart, including the preoperative orders. Dwight had been put on nothing by mouth at midnight, and an hour before surgery he was to get an injection of Demerol and atropine. Luckily I had index cards for these medications in my metal file box. I quickly pulled out the cards and reviewed them before Miss Carpenter had a chance to ask questions. I made a mental note that children often have a flushed face after receiving atropine. This was a common side effect and nothing to worry about. Once I had reviewed everything, I began to notice my anxiety level going up just thinking about giving an injection to a six-year-old.

Dwight was wide-awake, sitting up in bed and talking with his roommate. He had big blue eyes and blond hair that stuck straight up on the crown of his head. He was missing his two bottom front teeth.

"Good morning, Dwight. My name is Miss Swan."

He glanced over at me and resumed his conversation with the boy about his age in the other bed.

"What's your name?" I asked his roommate.

"James."

"How old are you?"

"Seven. Dwight and me are getting our tonsils out," he said proudly.

"I know."

"You do?" he said looking surprised.

"Yeah. A little birdie told me."

Both boys giggled.

A staff nurse walked into the room and pulled the curtain around James's bed. I could hear the nurse tell James she was going to give him a bath and then an injection so he would be ready for surgery.

Dwight looked at me with his big blue eyes and asked, "Do I have to get a shot?"

"Yes," I said.

He contorted his face and said, "Ugh."

"Sounds like you don't like shots."

"I don't!" he said emphatically.

"I'm going to check your temperature and blood pressure. After that, I'll help you get a bath."

"I know how to wash myself," he said.

"Well then, I'll just get everything ready for you, and when you're done, I'll wash your back."

I checked his vital signs, which were normal. After procuring a basin of water, I handed him a bar of soap, a washcloth, and towel, and said, "Go ahead and wash yourself. I'll come back in a few minutes and wash your back. Wash real good, and don't forget to wash behind your ears," I said jokingly.

Ten minutes later, I returned to his room.

"I'm done," he said proudly.

"Let me check behind your ears." I pulled each ear forward and pretended like I was carefully examining the area. "I don't see any bugs," I said.

Dwight giggled.

After I scrubbed his back, I handed him his toothbrush and toothpaste. "Go ahead and brush your teeth, I'll give you a little water to rinse your mouth. Don't swallow any. Spit it in this basin," I said as I placed an emesis basin on his bedside table.

"Okay," he said.

"Pinky promise?"

"Yes," he said as we entwined our pinky fingers.

He brushed his teeth and used the water to rinse his mouth.

When he finished, I said, "I'm impressed. You did a great job."

A few minutes later, Dwight's mother arrived. She was allowed to stay with him until he went to surgery, which was one of the few exceptions to the rules for visiting outside of visiting hours.

Miss Carpenter met me in the medication room to prepare Dwight's preoperative medications. The interrogation began. "What is Dwight's hemoglobin?" she asked.

I wasn't off to a good start and was feeling angry with myself for not knowing the answer. I had looked through Dwight's chart earlier but couldn't remember.

"Go get his chart," she said matter-of-factly with no hint of disappointment in her voice.

I looked up the information and returned saying, "Twelve point nine."

"What should it be before surgery?" she asked

"I believe it should be eleven or higher."

"That's right," she said. "How much does he weigh?"

75

"Forty-two pounds."

"Why is he getting Demerol and atropine?"

"To sedate him and dry up the secretions in his mouth and respiratory tract."

I prepared the medication using a 25-gauge one-inch needle.

"Where are you going to give the injection?" she asked.

"In his thigh," I said.

I had researched giving injections to children and knew the buttocks were not good sites. There was a greater danger of hitting the sciatic nerve in children. I felt proud knowing the correct site.

We walked to Dwight's room. I asked his mother to step out of the room while we gave the shot.

"Dwight, I need you to lie real still. I'm going to give your medicine in your leg," I said as I touched his thigh.

Miss Carpenter placed her hands on his thigh and was prepared to hold his leg still if he tried to move. I administered the shot and uttered a sigh of relief. Miss Carpenter looked at me and smiled. Dwight hadn't moved a muscle.

"I thought you told me you didn't like shots," I said.

"I don't."

"You were really brave. I'll get your mom." I told Dwight. "She can stay with you while you rest."

I checked in on Dwight thirty minutes later and found him fast asleep, holding his mother's hand.

"Why are his cheeks so red?" his mother whispered.

"The medicine I gave him causes that. It's nothing to be concerned about."

At a quarter to ten in the morning, Dwight was whisked off to surgery, and he returned at one thirty. He was groggy and indifferent to my presence. As soon as I finished checking him, he drifted back to sleep. His mom arrived at two in the afternoon for visiting hours.

I handed her a cup of ice chips. "He can have a few of these if he wants something when he wakes up."

I checked his vital signs one more time before leaving at two thirty. We spent the final hour of our day in a post conference. During this time, my classmates and I shared information about our patients and learned from all our experiences.

Dwight was awake the next morning when I went to his room to check his vital signs. James was still sleeping. I brought Dwight his breakfast, consisting of Jell-O and pear juice.

After taking a sip of juice and a spoonful of Jell-O, he said, "I'm not hungry."

"Okay. I'll leave your juice here. You can take some sips when you're ready. I'll be back a little later to help you get a bath."

When I returned, I noticed his juice was untouched. "Aren't you getting thirsty?"

"Yeah, but it hurts to swallow."

"I can give you some aspirin."

Miss Carpenter watched as I prepared some baby aspirin.

Just when I thought I wouldn't be asked any questions because aspirin was a common over-the-counter drug, Miss Carpenter asked, "What are the symptoms of aspirin poisoning?"

"Tinnitus," (ringing in the ears) "dizziness, nausea, and vomiting."

I hadn't remembered nausea and vomiting specifically, but it seemed like all the drugs could cause this, so I included it.

"Are there any other symptoms?" she asked.

Retrieving the card on aspirin from my file box and reading from it I said, "Hearing and vision disturbances. The signs of more severe poisoning include hyperventilation, fluctuations in blood pressure, confusion, fever, coma, and death."

"What about bleeding?"

"If large amounts of aspirin are taken it decreases the prothrombin time, which could result in bleeding," I said.

"How is he to take the baby aspirin?"

"I'll tell him to let it melt in his mouth."

Thirty minutes after Dwight took the aspirin, I brought him an orange Popsicle.

"Would you like this?" I asked while holding it up in front of his face.

His eyes popped wide open. He seized the Popsicle from my hand and licked it until it was gone.

Dwight fell asleep a few minutes later and slept on and off the rest of the morning. His lunch consisted of cool broth, Jell-O, and ice cream. I thought he would be excited seeing the ice cream. He ate three spoonfuls and pushed his tray away.

I talked with Dwight's mom during her visit.

She said, "Last night, he didn't want to swallow. Is he doing better today?"

"A little. He had a sip of pear juice, some Jell-O, a Popsicle, and a few bites of ice cream. I gave him some aspirin, and he did a little better swallowing. I'll remind the nurses to give him some more before dinner."

Looking at Dwight I asked, "Would you like another popsicle? We have orange and grape."

"Grape," he said.

"That sounds good," I said.

I brought it to his room and left so he and his mom could visit.

Both Dwight and his roommate were discharged from the hospital the next morning. I stopped by to say goodbye before going to meet Henry, who I would be taking care of that day.

Henry was a two-year-old diagnosed with LTB (laryngotracheobronchitis), commonly called croup. He looked tiny lying in his crib inside a croup tent. The tent was cooled by packing ice in a reservoir on the back of the device, and a cool mist was added to the circulating air in the tent. His breathing was rapid, and he made a high-pitched noise with every inspiration, making him sound like a squeaky wheel. I lowered the side rail and pulled up the front of the tent from under the sheet that was holding it in place.

"Good morning, Henry. My name is Miss Swan."

He looked at me and started to sit up, bringing on spasms of coughing. If I hadn't been looking at Henry, I would have thought there was a seal barking in his room. He looked and sounded pitiful.

"You're soaking wet. Are you cold?" I asked.

Henry nodded his head yes.

"I'll be right back," I said as I tucked the front of the tent back under the sheet.

I brought back a clean sheet, a soft warm bath blanket, and a fresh gown. When I touched Henry, it felt like he was burning up. I checked his temperature. It was 103.8 degrees Fahrenheit, and his respirations were thirty per minute.

"I'm going to leave again and get some medicine for you," I told Henry.

Miss Carpenter was in the medication room with another student. I waited until she finished and said, "I want to get Henry's medicines for this morning. He has a temperature of 103.8 degrees Fahrenheit. He hasn't had any aspirin since 2:00 a.m."

"What meds does Henry get this morning?"

"Some Benylin cough syrup and a multivitamin. I plan to give him some aspirin also."

"What is his hemoglobin?"

Once again, I did not know, but I was beginning to see a pattern. As I went to get Henry's chart, I thought, *This is the last time I won't know my patient's hemoglobin level.*

I poured the sticky Benylin cough syrup from the stock bottle into a plastic medicine cup. Miss Carpenter reminded me to get a wet paper towel and clean the top of the stock medicine bottle before putting the lid back on, to prevent it from getting crusted with the sticky medicine. I appreciated that bit of advice, especially when struggling to get a cap off a bottle that hadn't been wiped clean. Henry chewed the multivitamin and aspirin easily. When I tried to give him the cough syrup, he pressed his lips together tightly and shook his head from side to side. No amount of coaxing changed his mind. Henry was sick and weak, but he sure was feisty.

"Pick him up and sit in the chair. I'll hold his head and arms. Put his legs between your legs and hold them tightly, pinch his nostrils with one hand. He'll have to take a breath. When he does, pour the medicine in his mouth and press his lips together," Miss Carpenter said.

I didn't like the sounds of that, but I did as she'd instructed and got the medicine in his mouth, pressed his lips together, and waited for him to swallow. Once he swallowed the medicine, I let go of his lips. Henry began screaming and coughing, and big tears rolled down his cheeks. I placed him over my shoulder and patted his back gently before putting him back in the croup tent, all the while feeling like a mean old grinch. He rested his head on his pillow and coughed between sobs. I left his room to get a bucket to drain the water in the croup tent reservoir and refill it with ice.

The oxygen tank gauge needle was in the red zone, almost to the E, meaning empty, so after filling the reservoir, I left to find Miss Carpenter. "I need to replace the oxygen tank," I told her. "I've seen how it's done, but I haven't done it."

"I'll have an orderly help you," she said.

Even with the orderly watching and directing me, I was anxious, having heard scary tales of oxygen tanks blowing up and flying around the room.

I cracked the new tank by opening the valve to blow out any debris before attaching the gauge. There was a loud swish, and I flinched.

The orderly laughed and asked, "Why did that frighten you?"

"I've heard too many horror stories of tanks exploding."

"Nothing's going to happen if you follow the steps," he said in a soothing voice.

By the time I got back to Henry's room, he had fallen asleep. I changed out the oxygen tank quietly, and Henry slept through it all.

I let him sleep about an hour before giving him his breakfast and bath and rechecking his temperature. It had dropped to 99.8 degrees Fahrenheit, and the cough syrup was working. When I finished, he went back to sleep until lunchtime.

After lunch, I changed his gown and sheets, drained and refilled the croup tent reservoir with ice, and rechecked his temperature. It had climbed back up to 102.4 degrees Fahrenheit. I gave him more aspirin and the dreaded cough syrup.

Henry's mom arrived at two in the afternoon. She lifted the tent from under the cover and gave him a hug and a kiss. Henry grabbed her around the neck, sobbed, and wouldn't let go. I felt like crying too.

Before leaving for the day, I did a final check on Henry and got him a dry gown and sheets, replaced the oxygen tank, and filled the reservoir with fresh ice.

I took care of Henry the next day and the following week. His breathing gradually improved, and I almost became proficient at working with a croup tent. Henry never learned to like the cough syrup, and I never learned how to work with my head inside the tent without emerging with my nursing cap hanging off the side of my head. By the end of the week, Henry was laughing at me.

Jennifer, the first and only child of Mr. and Mrs. Martin, was a frail, thin seven-month-old baby. Dr. Young had admitted her to the hospital with the diagnoses of failure to thrive and respiratory infection. Scanning her chart revealed Dr. Young suspected Jennifer had cystic fibrosis. He told Jennifer's parents he wanted to admit her to treat the respiratory infection and run some tests to see if he could find a reason for Jennifer's repeated respiratory problems. He did not tell them what he suspected.

I met Jennifer's parents when they arrived for visiting hours.

"How's she doing?" they inquired.

"She's had a pretty good morning. She is eating well, drinking her formula, and swallowing her Terramycin like a real trooper," I responded.

Mrs. Martin lifted Jennifer from her crib and said, "Hi, Jennifer. It's your mommy. I've missed you so much."

Jennifer smiled and stared at her mother.

Dad stroked Jennifer's head and said, "I love you," as Mom cuddled her.

"I read that she is your only child," I said.

"Yes. She's our one and only," Mom said tenderly. "We've been worried about her. Something's wrong. She keeps getting respiratory infections, and she's not gaining weight like she should. Just like you said, she eats well, but she's so thin. About the time we think she's doing a little better, she gets another infection."

While listening to Mrs. Martin, my thoughts wandered back to one of my high school classmates. She had been admitted to the hospital with pneumonia and had died a few days later. After her death, I learned she had cystic fibrosis; her friends said she was lucky to have lived as long as she did. I didn't know much about the disease. I knew, after caring for Jennifer, it was time for me learn all I could.

I found a quote from the 1700s: "Woe is the child who tastes salty from a kiss on the brow, for he is cursed, and soon must die." Symptoms of cystic fibrosis were coughing and wheezing; poor growth despite a good appetite; frequent lung infections; and bulky, fatty stools. No wonder Dr. Young suspected cystic fibrosis. I decided to kiss Jennifer the next time I saw her.

Cystic fibrosis is hereditary, and both parents must have the recessive gene in order to pass it on. If both parents have the recessive gene, chances are one in four their child will have cystic fibrosis, and the life expectancy is five years. For some unknown reason, water and salt cannot move in and out of certain cells, especially the lungs and pancreas, which results in a thick, sticky mucus clogging air passages and pancreatic ducts. Stopped up respiratory ducts cause breathing problems and repeated respiratory infections. Clogged pancreatic ducts prevent digestive enzymes from reaching the small intestine to break down food for absorption, resulting in malnutrition. In the 1950s, it was discovered there was an increased salt content in the sweat of people with cystic fibrosis. Sweat tests were developed to measure salt content and make a diagnosis of cystic fibrosis.

I saw Dr. Young the next morning and asked if he was planning to do a sweat test. He was impressed when I asked the question, so I told him I had read about cystic fibrosis last night after caring for Jennifer.

"I didn't know much about it before last night," I said. "I kissed her forehead this morning, and she tasted salty."

"Yes. I kissed her at the office. That's when I suspected cystic fibrosis," he said.

When he finished writing in her chart, he handed it to me. I spotted the order for a sweat test. Once the sweat test results were back, the diagnosis of cystic fibrosis was confirmed.

Dr. Young met with Jennifer's parents. "They were distraught and shocked to learn they were carriers," he told me. "I went over my plan of treatment with them, and when I finished, they asked about her prognosis. I told them we would have to wait and see how Jennifer responded to treatment. They'll most likely ask you and the other staff the same questions. We all need to be on the same page and give them consistent answers. Have them ask me if you aren't sure what to say."

"Okay," I said.

Dr. Young wrote orders for a croup tent and postural drainage four times a day. The mist in the tent helped thin the thick mucus, and the postural drainage propelled the mucus up and out of the airway.

Just before lunchtime, after Jennifer had been in the croup tent for several hours, I performed postural drainage by cupping my hand and tapping on her back and making a vibrating motion with my fingers. About every five minutes, I repositioned Jennifer and repeated the process to loosen mucus in another area of her lungs. Jennifer coughed up thick, sticky mucus during the treatment.

Just as Dr. Young predicted, the parents asked me questions about Jennifer's prognosis and treatment. I told them, "I'm learning a little more about cystic fibrosis every day, and there is new information being discovered each year. I think the treatments are improving, and it all depends how Jennifer responds to the treatments."

They seemed to be satisfied and hopeful with my answer. Before discharge, Jennifer's parents were instructed to keep Jennifer in a mist tent at night and taught how to do postural drainage.

About a year after I had taken care of Jennifer, I learned that Mr. and Mrs. Martin filed for a divorce. I was saddened to hear this news and wondered if their decision was made from the stress of having a chronically ill child and/or the knowledge that they both had the recessive gene for cystic fibrosis.

While I was caring for three-year-old Samantha, who had extensive damage to her throat and esophagus after drinking Drano, Miss Carpenter asked me to admit four-year-old Ted, who would be arriving in about thirty minutes. I hurriedly prepared Samantha's lunch of pureed foods. Samantha spotted me carrying the tray and lifted her gown to expose the feeding tube stuck through her abdomen directly into her stomach.

"Are you hungry?"

She nodded her head. Samantha couldn't speak or swallow. It was difficult not to feel sorry for her, but we had been told to empathize with our patients, not sympathize. This required figuratively placing myself in her shoes and experiencing her feelings. I wanted to cry.

"Good. Let's start with the bananas. They smell yummy."

Samantha heeded my every move. When the feeding was finished, she pulled the gown back over the tube.

"Look what I found on your tray! It's a book about *The Three Little Pigs*."

Samantha snatched the book from my hands and began turning the pages.

"You can keep it."

She smiled and hugged the book.

Time to find out more about Ted, who I would be admitting. Dr. Sweeney saw him in his office and wanted to run some tests; he suspected Ted had a blood disorder, possibly leukemia. For the second time this morning, I found myself fighting back tears.

Ted and his mother arrived on the unit at 11:40 a.m. Taking a deep breath and swallowing hard, I gathered the papers and turned to go meet Ted. Miss Carpenter patted me gently on the shoulder. Was it obvious how fragile I felt?

Ted was sitting on Mom's lap with his head leaning on her shoulder.

"Good morning, Mrs. Lucas. Hi, Ted. My name is Miss Swan."

Mrs. Lucas said, "Hello."

Ted looked at me with his big green eyes and pushed harder against Mom's body.

"Ted, how old are you?"

He buried his face in Mom's chest.

"Don't you feel like talking?" I asked.

With his head still buried, he shook his head.

"Okay. I'll ask your mom a few questions. What prompted you to take Ted to the doctor this morning?"

"For the past month, Ted has been extremely tired and not wanting to do anything but lie on the couch and watch TV. Yesterday, I noticed bruises on his arms and legs." Her voice quivered, and she lovingly stroked his leg.

"Has he had a fever?"

"Not that I know of."

"How's his appetite?"

"Poor. He's lost weight and looks pale."

"Any pain?"

She looked at Ted and asked if he hurt anywhere. Ted shook his head.

"Have you noticed anything else?" I asked.

"He's had several bad nosebleeds."

After finishing the questions, Mrs. Lucas helped him put on a hospital gown, and I examined Ted. He was forty-one inches tall, weighed thirty-one pounds, and had a normal blood pressure, but his temperature was slightly elevated at 100.2 degrees Fahrenheit. There were several large bruises on his arms and legs, and upon closer examination, small pinpoint bruises could be detected.

Mrs. Lucas asked, "What's next?"

"Dr. Sweeney ordered some blood tests. Someone from the lab should be here shortly."

Ted was exhausted and lay on the bed and closed his eyes.

"You can say goodbye to Ted. Visiting hours are from 2:00 to 4:00 p.m. this afternoon and 6:30 p.m. to 8:00 p.m. tonight."

Mrs. Lucas leaned over and gave Ted a hug and a kiss and said, "I'm going to leave and eat some lunch, and then I'll be back."

Ted opened his eyes briefly as she said goodbye to him. Within five minutes, Ted was fast asleep.

I joined some of my classmates in the cafeteria. Joanne was excited, having just seen the birth of twins, and Lois had been working in surgery and had seen a gallstone removed that looked like half of a hot dog.

She said, "I don't think I'll ever eat another hot dog."

Everyone laughed.

By the time I returned to the unit, my spirits were lifted.

Samantha's mom came during visiting hours. She held Samantha and read *The Three Little Pigs*. Ted's mom sat at his bedside and watched Ted as he slept. Both moms looked exhausted.

Ted's blood test came back, revealing a low red blood cell and platelet count and a high number of white blood cells. Dr. Sweeney ordered a bone marrow test after reviewing the results and planned to do the aspiration in the morning at eight o'clock.

Miss Carpenter met with me after morning report and said, "It's time for Ted to get an injection of Demerol. He needs to get it thirty minutes before Dr. Sweeney gets here. Even with the Demerol, Ted will feel pain."

Dr. Sweeney arrived promptly at 8:00 a.m. Mrs. Noe, the staff RN, and I gathered everything needed and headed to Ted's room.

Ted, still sleeping, did not hear us walk in his room. Mrs. Noe watched me unwrap the tray and pour an antiseptic solution into the sterile bowl filled with cotton balls. I heard someone entering the room and turned to look. It was Miss Carpenter.

She got close to me and whispered, "How do you know someone didn't contaminate your tray? Never take your eyes off an open sterile tray."

"Do I need to get a new tray?"

"Not this time. No one touched it."

Feeling relieved and humbled, I said, "Thanks."

Dr. Sweeney arrived, spoke briefly with Ted, positioned him on his side exposing his right hip, and donned a pair of sterile gloves. He lifted a sterile syringe and needle from the tray and asked for Xylocaine. The Xylocaine bottle was not sterile, so I cleaned the rubber stopper on the bottle and held it as he pushed the needle through the stopper and drew up the medicine.

Mrs. Noe instructed me to hold Ted's legs, and she placed one of her hands above his hip and the other on his shoulder.

Dr. Sweeney told Ted, "I'm going to wash your hip. It's going to feel cold."

He grasped a cotton ball from the basin using sterile forceps and scrubbed Ted's hip before saying, "You're going to feel a bee sting."

After injecting the Xylocaine, he waited for a couple of minutes before telling Ted he would feel some pressure and to lie still. Dr. Sweeney used a special needle with a stylus and pushed it through Ted's skin and into the bone.

Ted tried to squirm and started to cry. I wanted to scoop him up in my arms and comfort him.

"You're doing well," Mrs. Noe told Ted.

Holding Ted's legs tightly as the little boy tried to pull away from the needle, Dr. Sweeney removed the stylus, connected the needle to a syringe, and aspirated some bone marrow. The marrow was a red liquid, not the thick white-pink marrow I was accustomed to seeing in beef bones.

When done, Dr. Sweeney placed a pressure dressing over the site and said, "Try to keep him quiet and resting for the next hour. I'll leave an order for something for pain. He can have it every six hours if needed."

I sat down and placed my hand on Ted's shoulder until he fell back asleep.

The bone marrow examination confirmed the diagnosis of acute lymphocytic leukemia. Dr. Sweeney planned to tell Ted's parents and go over his plan of care.

It had been less than twenty years since the medical community had discovered cancer could be treated with drugs, and Methotrexate was one of the first drugs used. The US National Cancer Institute was founded in 1953, and in 1955, the first federal program was financed to promote drug research for cancer. The most common cancer in young children was acute lymphocytic leukemia, and the majority of children died within three to four months after diagnosis.

Ted's parents were devastated. When they visited with Ted, they acted as if everything was fine and told Ted he was going to get medicine to help him get well. After leaving Ted's room, Mrs. Lucas broke down in tears and nearly collapsed in her husband's arms.

Ted began receiving high doses of prednisone, Methotrexate, and 6-mercaptopurine and experienced all the usual side effects—nausea, vomiting, chills, and hair loss. He looked adorable with his chubby cheeks (a side effect from the prednisone), bald head, and big green eyes. I tried to forget about his prognosis.

My assignment changed the next week, but I kept tabs on Samantha and Ted. Samantha was discharged doing well, and a public health nurse was scheduled to make regular visits. She was expected to live. Her recovery would be long and involve several surgeries to reconstruct her esophagus. Ted was discharged after completing chemotherapy but was readmitted three weeks later. The leukemia was aggressive, and Ted died within a few days. I snuck into the bathroom and bawled.

At birth, Eric was a full-term, healthy baby, but Mom noticed he was different from his siblings. He regurgitated frequently, stayed hungry, ate voraciously, and was losing weight. Mom became alarmed and took Eric to the pediatrician when Eric heaved, spewing stomach contents several feet across the floor. The pediatrician sent him to the hospital and ordered a surgical consult.

Six-week-old Eric was lying in his crib devouring his fist. I had just finished bathing him when the surgeon, Dr. Levine, arrived carrying a baby bottle of sterile water and a flashlight. He gently removed Eric's little white shirt to expose his stomach and palpated his abdomen.

"He looks hungry. Give him some water to drink," he said, looking directly at me.

Eric began drinking the water I offered ravenously. Dr. Levine crouched down to eye level with Eric's tummy and shined the light across his abdomen.

"There they are. I can see peristaltic waves moving left to right across his stomach. Feel right here," he said, pointing to the right upper quadrant of Eric's abdomen.

I placed my fingers where Dr. Levine was pointing.

"Do you feel anything?" he asked.

"Yes. A lump about the size of a marble."

"That's the pylorus, the sphincter that food passes through from the stomach to the intestines. It's thickened, and his formula can't get through. Eric has pyloric stenosis. The peristaltic waves will get more forceful, trying to push it through the pylorus. Eventually the water will fly out of his mouth.

"Some doctors try to correct this condition by treating it medically, using formula thickened with cereal and hoping it can push its way through and stretch the opening. I don't like trying that because, if it doesn't work, Eric will get weaker and more dehydrated. I'll talk with the pediatrician and get Eric on tomorrow's surgery schedule. It's simple surgery. I'll split the pyloric sphincter lengthwise, being careful not to cut the whole way through it. This enables it to stretch open so Eric's stomach can empty its contents. The biggest risk for Eric is being put under anesthesia; my part is easy."

It was time to feed Eric. He sucked voraciously on the nipple and cried when it was pulled out of his mouth so he could be burped. I stayed with Eric after his feeding, watching waves moving like small ripples in a lake growing larger and larger and culminating with projectile vomiting. The formula shot out of his mouth, landing on the floor in the middle of the room. After vomiting, Eric was ready to eat again.

The next morning, I prepared tiny Eric for surgery by checking his vital signs, weighing and bathing him, and giving his preoperative medication. Dr. Levine had originally written an order to insert a nasogastric tube before going to surgery but changed his mind and decided to wait until Eric was in the operating room before inserting the tube. Eric was ready for surgery by eight thirty, and his parents were sitting by his side. I uttered a silent prayer before leaving his room.

My thoughts quickly turned to Richard, a nine-month-old recently diagnosed with hemophilia. While pulling himself up on the furniture and attempting to take a few steps, Richard had fallen, banging his head on the coffee table and his knee on the hard floor. Frantically, his parents had rushed him to the emergency room, and subsequently he had been admitted.

Blood normally clots in three to six minutes. With hemophilia it can take up to an hour for a clot to form, due to an antihemophilic globulin deficiency. There was no additional information on antihemophilic globulin, so I concluded it was a clotting substance found in the blood. There were several types of hemophilia. Hemophilia A was cited as the most common type. Treatment included transfusions of fresh blood or plasma, since the globulin lost its activity rapidly in stored blood or plasma. Richard received fresh plasma shortly after his admission to the ward.

The main concerns were preventing further injury and monitoring for signs of increased intracranial pressure. There was a net over the top of Richard's crib, and the sides were padded with blankets attached securely to the rails. The ice bag on his knee had slipped off. Shades of deep purple, red, and yellow covered his humongously swollen knee. My heart flipped, and with hands trembling, I gently laid the ice pack in place, hoping his head injury was less traumatic. He lay still with eyes closed and lips pursed. His cheek twitched when stroked—good sign, not in a coma. He squeezed his eyelids as I pulled them open and found his pupils were equal and reacted to light.

Miss Carpenter walked in and asked, "How's he doing?"

"His knee looks awful, but he's responsive. His pupils are equal and react to light. He resisted when I pulled his eyelids open, and he hasn't had any vomiting."

"Did you check for a bulging fontanel?" She was referring to the soft spot on an infant's head where skull bones have not yet fused together. With increased intracranial pressure, the soft spot will bulge.

"Yes. His head felt normal. No visible lumps, bulging, or bruising."

"When you are ready, write down everything you plan to chart. I want to review it before you enter it in the chart."

"Okay."

After completing Richard's bath and feeding, I jotted down my notes. Miss Carpenter approved my notes, with instructions to add the strength of his sucking and a description of his cry.

My other patient, Eric, was brought back to his room around noon and was propped on his right side to help the digestive juices empty from his stomach and prevent aspiration if he vomited. Dr. Levine ordered a Down's regimen to be started four hours after surgery if Eric had no vomiting. There were written instructions ordering increasing amounts of glucose water to be given every thirty minutes; on the fourth hour, skimmed milk was added, and the frequency of feedings decreased to every hour. I would be leaving for the day before his first feeding, and by the time of my return, he would be receiving an ounce of skimmed milk and a dram (seventy-four drops) of glucose water.

Morning report revealed Richard had no signs of increased intracranial pressure. He was eating without problems, moving about more in his crib, and crying when he tried to move his restrained leg. His knee still looked grotesque. Repeated injuries could result in joint damage. His parents were taught to have him wear knees pads and a helmet once he was up and about.

Eric vomited one time and the amount of his feedings was decreased temporarily. I cuddled him in my arms during his feedings, which he tolerated with no additional episodes of vomiting.

Seven-year-old Ann was admitted for treatment of sickle-cell crisis. She was diagnosed with sickle-cell disease when she was five months old and had been hospitalized numerous times through the years.

Her first words to me were "I have sickle-cell disease."

"What do you know about it?"

"I got it from my mom and dad. There's something wrong with my red blood cells. Mom said they look like the letter C," she explained, referring to the sickle shape, "and get stuck in my veins. That causes pain. They should look like the letter O."

"Were you having pain when you came to the hospital?"

"My chest, legs, and tummy hurt. I was crying."

"They must have hurt really bad."

"Yes."

"What did the doctor do when you got to the hospital?"

"He said I probably had an infection that caused me to get sick. My throat was red. He gave me medicine to stop the pain and put this needle in me. He said he was giving me something to drink in my veins to help make the pain go away."

"Did it help?"

"A little. I stopped crying."

"Do you know what veins are?"

"Yes. Blood runs through them. I miss my mom and dad."

"You've had to be away from them a lot. How many times have you been in the hospital?"

She squinted, raised an eyebrow, and said, "I don't know."

"Too many times," I said.

She smiled and said, "Right." Her two front upper teeth were missing.

"Do you know what I think?"

"No," she replied.

"You're adorable and smart."

"That's what Mom says."

My other patient, Louie, was three and a half years old. He was scheduled for surgery to correct strabismus (crossed eyes). His eye doctor had tried to correct the strabismus by having Louie wear a patch over his good eye, forcing him to use the weak eye in hopes it would strengthen the muscles. It didn't work, and a decision was made to take him to surgery to shorten and stretch some of the eye muscles.

Louie was admitted to the hospital two days before his scheduled surgery to prepare him for postoperative care. Each afternoon and evening, the nurses, with his parents present during visiting hours, covered both his eyes and restrained his arms. To my astonishment, arrangements were made for his mother to stay with him after surgery. A door was being opened for parents' involvement.

I talked about Louie and Ann during our post conference. My classmates were surprised how much seven-year-old Ann knew.

Clare asked, "Did she talk about her future?"

"She told me she was going to be a nurse when she grew up. I told her she would have to study hard, but she was smart and would be a good nurse."

Sherry asked, "Isn't the life expectancy short?"

"It is shorter than normal, but some children grow up to lead fairly normal lives and are able to work. I wanted to encourage her."

They were also amazed that Louie's mom could stay with him. The consensus was that progress was being made.

By the end of the next week, Ann and Louie were discharged. Louie's surgery had gone well. Once his eye was healed, he would be fitted for glasses. I pictured him with his big green eyes sparkling through the lenses. Maybe as he got older, the children would tease him and call him four eyes, but I didn't think that would bother Louie. He was a brave boy with loving parents who would always be there to support him.

It was time to leave pediatrics and move to Cleveland for my psychiatric rotation. I would miss the children. Exiting the unit for the final time, I was suddenly filled with gratitude for what I had learned and for being a healthy teenager.

PSYCHIATRIC NURSING

Just a year before I began my psychiatric nursing rotation, Ken Kesey, a graduate student working the night shift on a psychiatric ward, wrote *One Flew Over the Cuckoo's Nest.* It portrayed a ghastly picture of psychiatric nursing. I read the book a few months before going to Cleveland to study psychiatric nursing. It was a chilling reality. Or was it? Nurse Ratched was evil, treating her patients like pawns.

A nurse friend, JoAnne, described her student experience at Torrance State Hospital (Pennsylvania) in 1953, where the care was mainly custodial. She described patients screaming and clinging to the bars on the windows. I was appalled. Insulin shock, electroshock, prefrontal lobotomies, and cold baths were the primary treatments. Nursing students observed patients during bath and meal times, gave haircuts, and shaved patients who were not permitted to use a razor. On weekends, JoAnne played ball games and attended hospital dances with the patients. These activities were intended to help patients learn social skills.

While I was packing bags for the move to Cleveland, I began having memories of my Aunt Elsie, who I had not seen since 1950. At age eighteen, Robert, her oldest son, was drafted into the army and sent to the Korean battlefield. He was killed in action on September 19, 1950. A few weeks after his funeral, Aunt Elsie's neighbor witnessed her in the yard naked and talking incoherently. She summoned the police. Aunt Elsie was admitted to Massillon State Hospital and was still there. I found myself lamenting the loss and wondering how someone needed to be in a hospital for twelve years, especially my sweet Aunt Elsie. She remained there for an additional five years before being discharged in 1968.

Before departing for Cleveland, Mrs. Davis gave instructions: "Don't go out after dark, and go with a group in the daytime. Do not date the Negro orderlies, and don't believe them if they threaten not to help in a psychiatric emergency if you refuse a date. They will protect their jobs."

I accepted the instructions, ignoring the twinge in my gut.

In summer 1963, six of my classmates and I moved into the dormitory in the slums of Cleveland to start our three-month rotation at the Cleveland Psychiatric Institute (CPI). CPI was a receiving hospital for newly diagnosed patients with serious mental disorders. Following an average length of stay of four to six months, patients were discharged home or transferred to the Cleveland State Hospital for long-term care. The dormitory was connected to CPI and Cleveland Metropolitan General Hospital by a maze of tunnels. It was in these tunnels where I was introduced to cockroaches. During my three months there I was too scared to set foot outside the dormitory or hospital, day or night, except to hop in a car at the front door to go home for a weekend visit.

Students from nursing programs throughout the state of Ohio came to CPI and were in the dorm and classes with us. This was our first opportunity to intermingle. We shared experiences and learned how fortunate we were to be at the MB Johnson School of Nursing. Many programs used students for hospital staffing. Thanks to our director, Mrs. Davis, our program was dedicated to learning.

We learned about Sigmund Freud's psychoanalytic theory and repressed memories and Harry Stack Sullivan's interpersonal theory, stressing the power of personality development and defense mechanisms learned in childhood and carried into adult life. Most psychiatric problems were attributed to environmental factors, with the belief something had gone awry in the mother-child relationship. Hildegard Peplau, a nursing theorist, taught that therapy was in the nurse-patient relationship. Memorizing the information was easy; translating it into action was grueling.

Before starting my psychiatric nursing rotation, I had communicated well with my patients. On the psychiatric ward, learned therapeutic and non-therapeutic responses swirled around in my brain. Trying to figure out what to say left me lost for words the first few weeks on the unit.

Women and men were housed on separate units. My first clinical assignment was on the women's ward. Miss Jensen accompanied me to the unit, where Mrs. Garfield, the staff nurse, opened the door to the unit using a large metal key. More keys hung from a chain around her waist, jingling when she moved and reminding me I was locked in the unit. It gave me the heebie-jeebies.

Miss Black, in her mid-forties, had been at CPI for three months with a diagnosis of psychoneurotic depressive reaction with psychosis. Today, this would be called major depression. I was to designate a thirty-minute period of time each day to do a process recording of our conversation, writing down everything we said and noting Miss Black's nonverbal communication and my feelings.

In the evenings, I analyzed my notes and identified defense mechanisms used by Miss Black, as well as my therapeutic and non-therapeutic responses, along with suggestions for better responses. At the end of each week, I handed over my recordings with my analyses to my instructor for review. They were returned covered in red ink. My analyses were good, but most of my responses were horrible according to Miss Jensen. I struggled with this week after week, seemingly getting nowhere.

Most of what I learned about Miss Black was by reading her chart. During our time together, she had very little to say. Each day at our designated time, I sat in a chair holding my notebook and pen and waiting for Miss Black to arrive. She would arrive promptly for each scheduled meeting, neatly groomed and dressed in a skirt, blouse, nylons, and shiny black shoes. Without fail, before sitting down, she would arrange her chair directly in front of me. Sitting in an upright position with her feet planted firmly on the floor and hands folded in her lap, she would look at me with a half smile and piercing brown eyes.

"Good morning, Miss Black. What would you like to talk about today?"

Silence. Three minutes passed. Getting frustrated and thinking there would be no conversation to analyze, I said, "Tell me about yourself."

"What do you want to know?"

"I would like to know more about you. What do you think about?"

There was more silence before she asked, "Think about what?"

"What are you thinking as you sit here this morning?"

"Nothing."

"Nothing?"

She cast her eyes toward the floor and remained silent. We spent the rest of our time in silence.

When our time was up I said, "It's time to go. I'll see you tomorrow at the same time."

She got up and slowly walked away with her head down.

Day after day, we spent our time together mainly in silence. Different opening statements produced the same results. I was puzzled and wondered why she showed up promptly just to sit and say nothing.

In my classes, I was horrified to learn that, in the past, patients had been kept in dark dungeons and chained to the walls. Many forms of treatment were tried through the centuries, including chiseling the skull to let the devil escape, relentlessly swinging patients in a chair to shake out the madness, placing patients in a box with holes and submerging it in water until the bubbling stopped, bloodletting, removing body parts, and giving ice baths. Nearly all these practices, at the time they were introduced, were thought to be revolutionary in the treatment of the mentally ill.

The most common treatments at CPI were electroshock therapy (EST) and drugs to calm and clear the thinking in patients with schizophrenic, depressive, manic depressive, and psychoneurotic reactions. Thankfully, insulin coma therapy and lobotomies were no longer used.

Insulin coma therapy had been used extensively in the United States since the late 1930s to induce insulin shock by administering insulin. The entire procedure was dangerous with a mortality rate of 1 to 10 percent. Electroshock therapy was thought to be safer, but patients suffered fractures, confusion, and severe memory loss.

In 1936, Dr. James W. Watts, a neurosurgeon, and Dr. Walter Freeman, a neurologist, began performing lobotomies in the United States. The procedure was used to destroy the frontal cortical tissue (the emotional center in the brain). The patient was given a tranquilizer prior to the procedure, and without anesthesia, small incisions were made near the top of the head on each side. After the surgeon drilled a hole through the skull, he would place a knife through the opening and wiggle it up and down and back and forth to destroy brain tissue. When the patient could no longer speak coherently, the surgery was stopped and considered successful.

In 1946, Dr. Freeman modified the procedure by using an instrument similar to an ice pick to tap through the thin bone of the eye socket into brain tissue. Once in place, the instrument was moved back and forth to destroy tissue, and the procedure was repeated through the other eye socket. It took about ten minutes to complete the entire procedure.

I was curious, yet tense the morning I was assigned to observe EST. Patients with schizophrenia or psychotic depression received EST several times a week for a total of ten to eighteen treatments. The patients were herded to an area where they waited their turn.

The first patient walked into the room, removed her slippers, climbed up on the narrow table, and lay down. She showed no emotion. The nurse placed an electrode on each side of her head and held them in place with a rubber strip secured around her head. She stuck a rubber mouthpiece in the patient's mouth to prevent biting the tongue during the convulsion. I was told to stand back and not touch any part of the table to prevent getting shocked.

Without any additional preparation, the doctor pressed a button on a machine and the patient had a grand mal seizure. When the jerking started, the nurse placed her hands lightly over the patient's legs to prevent them from flipping off the table. It took only a few moments before the convulsion stopped, and the patient was lifted onto a stretcher and wheeled to the recovery area.

I watched at least eight patients that morning and felt emotionally drained. Later that morning, I saw several of the patients on the ward. They were disoriented, looked dazed, and did not remember having had a treatment.

I wasn't enjoying my experiences. It was a totally different type of nursing.

Prior to the 1950s, drugs used in psychiatry were used to sedate or stimulate patients. Methylphenidate (Ritalin) was marketed in 1955 to treat hyperkinetic disorder of childhood, a disorder that was later renamed attention deficit hyperactivity disorder (ADHD).

In 1954, chlorpromazine (Thorazine), classified a major tranquilizer, was used in the treatment of schizophrenia and depression. Violent, delusional, and hallucinating patients became calmer and began thinking more clearly after receiving Thorazine. With this breakthrough, the use of electroshock therapy and lobotomies diminished.

Coinciding with the introduction of Thorazine was the development of two antidepressants—iproniazid and imipramine. It took ten years before these drugs were approved for the treatment of depression. Patients taking iproniazid began having sudden and dangerous spikes in their blood pressures because the drug blocked the breakdown of tyramine, an amino acid that helps to regulate blood pressure and found in many foods. Patients were put on low-tyramine diets, which restricted them from eating or drinking aged cheeses and wines, cured meats, some beers, and foods stored for long periods of time or not kept cold enough. Because of the inconvenience of the diet and the necessity of restricting foods they enjoyed, many chose not to take iproniazid.

Miss Black's medications included Ritalin to get her energized, Thorazine to treat the psychosis, and imipramine for her depression. I prepared her medications by obtaining them from gallon-sized bottles. No record was kept of any of the medications procured.

Miss Black swallowed her meds, opened her mouth, stuck out her tongue, and lifted it up without prompting so that I could inspect and run my finger around in her cheeks. The pills were gone. Thankfully, she had not tried to cheek them.

------------- ✚ -------------

It was my turn to supervise baths. Mrs. Garfield said, "Stay in the room at all times, help them get in and out of the tub, and keep them safe. Some patients may attempt to hurt themselves by drowning." Handing me a spray bottle filled with a disinfectant she added, "Use this to clean the tub between patients and prepare the water for the next patient. You need to fill the tub. Some patients, accidentally or intentionally, get the water too hot and scald themselves."

My mind began racing with thoughts about what to do if patients attempted to harm themselves and if I'd be physically strong enough to stop them. My fears were allayed upon spotting a call bell in the tub room.

My first patient arrived and began removing her clothes. As soon as the water was ready, she got in the tub with my assistance, and I sat in the chair beside the tub and started a conversation.

"Does it feel good to get in the water?"

"Yes."

"I enjoy a nice warm bath; it's refreshing."

"Yes," she said without looking at me.

I waited a minute or two as she scrubbed herself before asking, "What kinds of things do you like to do?"

"Jigsaw puzzles, but I'm not very good."

"Compared to who?"

"I don't know."

"Some puzzles are pretty hard and can take a lot of time just to find one piece. Do you usually get them put together?"

"Yes."

"It sounds to me like you have a lot of patience."

She did not say anything, so when it looked like she was finishing her bath I asked, "Are you ready for me to wash your back?"

"Yes."

When I finished, she said, "Thank you. That felt good."

"You're welcome. I enjoyed talking with you today."

She looked at me and smiled as she got out of the tub and dressed. I was pleased with the way it had gone and looked forward to the next patient's arrival. The morning went by quickly, and by the time the last patient finished, I found myself wishing there were more patients to help.

It was the day before a big test. Some of my classmates helped themselves to some Ritalin from the stock bottles on the wards. They thought it would improve their concentration while studying. After taking the medication, they got rowdy, running around the dormitory laughing and seemingly having a great time. Studying was the last thing on their mind; but they weren't as jovial and perky when they walked in the classroom to take their test. They later admitted taking the Ritalin had been a bad idea.

Halfway through the rotation, I was switched to the men's ward for the remainder of my stay. I said my goodbyes to the patients.

Miss Black said, "I'll miss you."

I was blown away. Never in a million years had I expected that. My attitude toward psychiatric nursing changed, and I understood that the therapy was in the nurse-patient relationship. It wasn't so much about what was said as it was about being there for the patient and showing respect.

The atmosphere on the men's unit was tense. Men were pacing in the halls, and the odor of urine permeated the unit. I told the RN, Mrs. Carlson, that I was surprised at the difference between the women's and men's wards.

"What is different?"

"The women were content to sit in the dayroom in silence or talk with each other occasionally. The men seem agitated."

"In the mornings, they are more restless. After taking their morning medications, they begin to mellow out."

"The other thing is that awful odor of urine."

"That is a problem. Some of the men get up at night and urinate on the walls or in the radiators. Housekeeping can't get rid of that putrid smell."

My assigned patient was fifty-seven-year-old Mr. Gentry, diagnosed with schizophrenic reaction, paranoid type. Two months earlier, he had been brought to the hospital because he thought he could fly. His wife had found him preparing to fly off an electric power company tower and called the police.

Prior to 1911, schizophrenia was called dementia praecox. The name was changed because it was not a dementia. Schizophrenia means "split mind," and even today this term is often misunderstood. The person does not have multiple personalities; he or she has fragmented thinking. Mr. Gentry had a delusion that he could fly and expressed his belief that God had given him this special ability. He became agitated and argumentative if anyone challenged his belief and would accuse them of trying to stop him from using his special power.

"Good morning, Mr. Gentry. My name is Miss Swan," I said as I introduced myself to him for the first time.

"Can you fly, too?"

I was puzzled by his response and said, "No, I can't fly. I don't know of any person who can."

"I can," he said matter-of-factly.

"I'm surprised. I've never heard of that."

He wrinkled his nose, raised a corner of his lip with a look of disgust, and walked over to a window in the dayroom. After watching him stare out the window for a few minutes, I walked up to him and asked, "What are you looking at?"

"The birds."

I looked out the window and saw a flock of sparrows perched on the telephone lines. "I see them."

"They'll fly away."

"I wonder where they go."

"To Florida," he said without hesitation.

"How do you know that?"

"I know everything about birds."

"Are you a member of the Audubon Society?"

"No, but I know everything," he said with a menacing smile that was making me feel uneasy.

I decided not to ask any more questions, saying, "I'll see you later."

I welcomed the weekend and seized the opportunity to go home. My brother Kevin had a new job working in a local golf ball manufacturing company. He lacked fine motor skills because of his cerebral palsy, so I was surprised and delighted that he'd landed the job. My mother said he had been acting strangely and withdrew to his room every day after work and on the weekends. In an attempt to get him out, I invited him to a movie. He refused.

"Ah, come on, it will be fun."

"I don't want to go," he said without opening the door to his room.

"May I come in?"

"No."

"Okay. I'm going downstairs. If you change your mind, let me know. I'll let you choose the movie. That sounds like a good deal to me."

He didn't emerge from his room until dinnertime and stayed only long enough to eat his meal in silence before returning to his room.

His behavior disturbed me. I wondered if he were a budding schizophrenic. He was the right age for symptoms to surface.

On my way back to Cleveland, I told my classmates my suspicions. They thought I was overreacting and reminded me what Miss Brown our med-surg instructor had told us about thinking we had the diseases we were studying. They teased me and said I was giving the disease to my brother. My fears were allayed.

The hall telephone was ringing. I didn't bother to get up since I had not received any phone calls since my arrival.

A peer popped her head through the doorway and said, "Nancy, it's for you."

As I walked to the phone, I asked myself who would be calling me.

"Hello."

"Hi. This is Larry Kerry." I froze. Larry was an orderly on the men's unit. "Do you know who I am?"

"Yes."

"Are you doing anything Saturday night?"

"I'll be studying for a big test on Monday."

"You'll need to take a break. I want to take you to a movie."

"I can't go."

"Sure you can. Don't you want to go out with me?"

"I really don't have the time. Besides, I have a steady boyfriend."

"You'll be sorry. We could have a good time."

"I'm still going to pass up the offer."

"Like I said, you'll be sorry." And he hung up.

Larry had just threatened me. I recalled our director, Mrs. Davis, telling us the orderlies would threaten us by implying they would not help us in an emergency if we refused to date them. Visibly shaking, I put down the receiver and returned to my room.

My roommate took one look at me and asked, "What's wrong?"

I relayed the details of the conversation and asked, "What should I do?"

"Tell Miss Jensen."

"What if that makes things worse?"

"How could that make it worse?"

"He could try to get back at me if I tell. I don't know what he'll do. I'm scared."

"Well I think you need to tell someone."

"I'll think about it."

I had a hard time concentrating on studying. Larry's threat was distracting me, and I couldn't decide what to do. By Tuesday morning, I was a nervous wreck. When I arrived on the ward, there he was standing in the hall. He just looked at me and smiled as I walked by. As the day progressed, I felt more at ease and convinced myself that nothing was going to happen.

Two weeks later, I was sitting with Mr. Gentry and five other patients at the dining room table. My assignment was to observe and record how much each patient ate and do a spoon count after the meal. Patients were known to sneak spoons out of the dining room and make sharp instruments with them. During the meal, I noticed Mr. Gentry stuffing food down in his shirt.

"That food will spoil," I told him. "You need to put it back on your plate."

"It's for the birds."

"The birds have plenty of food. Go ahead and put it back on the table."

"I have to feed them."

"I'm not allowed to let you take food out of the dining room. It will attract bugs and spoil if left in your room."

"I'm not going to leave it in my room. I told you it's for the birds," he bellowed, accentuating each word. He began grabbing handfuls of food and stuffing them into his shirt.

"Mr. Gentry, I know you are angry."

He leaped out of his chair and lunged toward me, yelling, "Miss Swan."

Larry and a patient who was sitting at the table were the first to my rescue. They grabbed Mr. Gentry by the arms. Two more orderlies appeared within seconds and held him back. Mr. Gentry fought and yelled. When he was subdued, they carried him out of the room. I was rattled.

Mrs. Carlson asked, "Are you okay?"

"I'm shook up, but I'll be okay. What's going to happen to Mr. Gentry?"

"They've taken him to seclusion on another ward. He won't be coming back to us."

"He scared me. Did you hear him screaming my name?"

"You know, he's always talking about birds."

Suddenly it clicked. Miss Swan. That's why he'd asked if I could fly.

I spent the afternoon talking with patients on the ward. Mr. Holcomb and I were sitting in the dayroom near a window having a casual conversation. Mr. Holcomb leaned forward and squinted as he peered through the window.

"Look at that man in the tree watching us. He was up there yesterday watching me. Do you know him?"

"I don't see him."

"He's right there near the top of the tree."

"I can't see anyone. Are you putting me on?"

Mr. Holcomb's muscles tensed up, and he glared at me.

"I'm sorry. I thought you were teasing."

He stood up and walked out of the room. I was relieved and didn't ask him to come back.

Mrs. Carlson gave me a new assignment. "Mr. Fentress will be an interesting patient. He has Huntington's chorea."

"I've never heard of it."

"There are nurses and doctors who never see a patient with Huntington's chorea."

I pulled his chart and read the notes. Mr. Fentress, a college graduate, had worked as a CPA until he began having memory and concentration problems. His wife got a job to support their family of four. Over the next year, Mr. Fentress had bouts of depression with angry outbursts. Two months ago, he had cut his wrist in a suicide attempt. His fifteen-year-old son had found him and sought help. Mr. Fentress was admitted to CPI and started on imipramine and Thorazine.

Mr. Fentress was sitting in the dayroom. He stood up and lost his balance when I walked up to him. I grabbed his arm to keep him from falling.

"I'm okay," he said and jerked his arm away.

We sat in the dayroom and talked. As we got to know each other, he confided he was no longer able to work and revealed his anguish over his inability to provide for his two boys and wife.

"I got depressed. I had hoped my boys would be able to go to college. My wife works long hours and only brings home enough money to pay the mortgage and buy the bare essentials. I have a life insurance policy and thought they would be better off if I were dead. You know, my boys have a fifty-fifty chance of having Huntington's chorea. If they get it, it will be my fault."

"Have you ever talked with your wife and boys about your concerns?"

"No, I think that would make it worse."

"How would talking with them make it worse?" I asked, remembering my response when my roommate suggested I talk with the head nurse about the orderly who had threatened me.

"I'm afraid to hear what they'll say. I think they resent my ineptitude. I'm a failure and a disappointment."

Mr. Fentress's words were slurred, and his eyebrows, mouth, and right shoulder twitched uncontrollably.

"What if they aren't feeling that way? Do you think it would be better having them tell you what they think?"

"Maybe."

"I believe an arrangement could be made to meet with your wife and doctor."

"I don't know about that."

"Could you give it some thought?"

"Okay."

"I'll check with you tomorrow."

I went to the library and found information about Huntington's chorea. Mr. Fentress had the classic symptoms, and he had been right when he'd said his sons had a chance of developing the disease. As the disease progressed, the twitching would get worse and more generalized and the patient would become demented and psychotic and would develop swallowing problems and might choke to death. The life expectancy was ten to thirty years after the onset of symptoms.

Mr. Fentress and I resumed our discussion from the previous day. He surprised me by saying he had told his doctor his burdens and asked for a meeting with his wife. His psychiatrist was in the process of making arrangements.

"I think you made the right decision. What are your feelings about it now that you decided to have a meeting?"

"Relieved and scared."

"That sounds normal. Not knowing is the hardest part. Have you thought about what you want to say?"

"Yes. Pretty much what I told you."

"I won't be seeing you until next Tuesday. Maybe you'll have the meeting before I see you again."

Early Tuesday morning, Judy and I got on the elevator en route to the cafeteria for breakfast. We were chatting when the elevator stopped with a sudden jolt. My anxiety level spiked. Judy began pressing the "open door" button repeatedly. When nothing happened, she pressed the buttons to other floors. Still no movement. At last, she pushed the red alarm button, and a loud bell sounded.

"Someone will surely hear that," I said. "I guess we'll just have to wait for them to get to us."

Judy pressed the button several more times while we waited.

"I wonder what's taking so long. I just want to get out of here."

Judy pushed the button again and let the bell ring for a long time. We waited a few minutes longer in dead silence; no sounds of voices, footsteps, or clanging tools.

Panicking, I said, "We have to get out of here."

"We have to stay calm," Judy said.

Once again, she began pressing buttons to the different floors. Finally the elevator moved and the door opened. It wasn't lined up with the floor. Directly in front of me was the wall of the elevator shaft. I looked up and saw the opening to a floor.

"Do you think it's safe to try to crawl out?"

"I don't know," Judy said.

"Maybe someone will hear us if we yell." I began yelling for help at the top of my lungs. Judy joined in.

No one responded to our cries.

"Let's try to get out."

"Okay," Judy said.

Judy helped to lift me so my hands could reach the floor at the door opening. I hoisted myself up and out of the elevator. Once I was safely out, I lay on the floor and reached down to grasp Judy's hands. I pulled her up until she could reach the floor with her hands and pull herself out of the elevator.

"That was scary. I kept thinking the elevator might move while we were crawling out. Let's find the receptionist," I said.

We walked down the stairs and went to the receptionist's desk. She was sitting behind her desk and smiled when we walked up to her.

"We've been stuck in the elevator. Did you hear the alarm?" I asked.

"Is that what I heard?"

I was infuriated. Constraining myself, I said, "It was the elevator alarm. It's been quite an ordeal. We managed to crawl out, but the elevator is still stuck."

"I'll call maintenance."

"Good. We have to go."

I walked away thinking she was just another warm body sitting at a desk.

Judy and I walked through the tunnel and passed the cafeteria on our way to the wards—no time for breakfast. Judy stopped when we got to the elevators and pushed a button.

"What are you doing?" I asked.

"What do you mean? I'm going to the ward."

"On the elevator?"

"Yes."

"Not me. I'm taking the stairs," I said and headed to the stairwell.

Mr. Fentress was standing by the door waiting for my arrival. "I didn't think you were coming."

"I'm running late. I'll meet you in the dayroom after I let the nurse know I'm here."

A moment later, I returned. "I'm back. Sorry to keep you waiting."

"I met with my wife yesterday. We had a good talk. She told me she loves me, and we'll get through this together. She had a lot of questions about the future and what to expect. Dr. Gammon told us he didn't know. He said every case is different, and we would deal with things as and if they occur."

"Did you talk about your boys?"

"Yes. They miss me and can't wait until I get home. My wife said they know I love them and couldn't understand why I tried to kill myself."

Mr. Fentress's mood was brighter, and he seemed to be more hopeful. I was thankful he was showing improvement emotionally, even though I knew it would be a rough road ahead. On my last day at CPI, plans were in progress for Mr. Fentress to be discharged. He was showing excitement about returning home. I wished I'd had the opportunity to meet his family, but visiting hours were on weekends only, plus the boys were too young to visit.

Staff was talking about changes occurring in psychiatric hospitals. President Kennedy had a special concern for mental illness and mental retardation and argued that these areas of health care had been neglected too long. His goal was to get patients out of state custodial institutions. His oldest sister, Rosemary, purportedly had an IQ of 60. And as she grew older, she began having mood swings and episodes of violent, angry outbursts. In 1941, her father, Joseph Kennedy, heard about a new procedure that helped to calm patients. Without his wife's knowledge, he had given consent for

Dr. Watts and Dr. Freeman to perform a lobotomy on twenty-three-year-old Rosemary. Due to incontinence and an infantile mentality following the procedure, Rosemary had to be institutionalized.

President Kennedy's administration decided no federal funds should go to state mental hospitals. He signed into law the Mental Retardation Facilities and Community Mental Health Center Construction Act of 1963. It mandated deinstitutionalization and sought to sweep away the dark age of institutional confinement. The staff was convinced this law would decrease the amount of monies available for mental hospitals to run efficiently. The hospital was already understaffed.

I packed my bags and moved back to my dorm room at MB Johnson. It felt good to be back. I cherished the moments I had taken for granted—going out for an evening stroll, stopping by a local store for some snacks, and weekend visits with my family.

Kevin's behavior continued to change. He had been a happy and mischievous child. When we looked through the family pictures, he often could be spotted in the background making funny faces. Once again, I asked Mom how he was doing. Besides staying in his room all weekend, she would hear him up in the night walking around the house. I wanted to tell her I thought he needed help, but I didn't want to alarm her or tell her what I thought was going on with him.

About two months after my arrival back at MB Johnson, Kevin had a total breakdown. Mom received a call from Kevin's boss asking her to come and get him. He had been found in one of the offices going through the cabinets, agitated and insisting there were keeping secret files. She took him to a doctor for an evaluation, and Kevin was diagnosed with paranoid schizophrenia. He was put on Mellaril but refused to take it most of the time. As time went on he became more agitated and threatening. Eventually he had to be hospitalized.

I stayed busy with my studies and didn't talk about it with my friends at school. Ashamed of having a mentally ill brother, I focused on my surgical rotation.

SURGERY AND RECOVERY ROOM

After returning from Cleveland at the end of summer 1963, I was ready to start my third and final year in nursing school. Before reporting to the operating room, I added the third black stripe to my nursing cap and sat admiring it with pride. I had been waiting for the day I could walk through those doors that had been off limits to me as a nursing aide while working in Central Supply. Today, I was joining the big league.

Miss Crowder, my new instructor, was waiting for my arrival and that of two of my classmates. After a brief greeting, she said, "Go put on surgical scrubs and cover your hair with a scrub cap."

We changed into the operating room garb and walked out of the dressing room looking like everyone else, with the exception of our eyes. Many of the female staff wore eye shadow, liner, and mascara. Then it dawned on me that their eyes were the only part of their face that could be seen in surgery.

The first thing we had to learn was how to get ready to assist in surgery. Miss Crowder took us to the sinks where staff scrubbed their hands. She demonstrated a surgical scrub using the knee controls for the water and a scrub brush for washing our forearms, hands, and under our fingernails for five minutes. There was a large clock mounted on the wall above the sinks for timing the scrub; it had to be accurate.

Miss Crowder explained, "If you were going into the operating room to assist, you would be wearing shoe covers and a mask. After scrubbing, hold your hands above your waist and go into the operating room, pick up a sterile towel and dry your arms and hands. The circulating nurse will assist you with putting on your gown and gloves. She'll tell you what to do. Remember, you are sterile only in the front from your neck down to your waist. Tomorrow you will observe one or two surgeries. Watch closely as each person enters the operating room and goes through this procedure. By the time you scrub in for surgery, you should know exactly what to do.

"Wear 100 percent cotton underwear tomorrow; nylon causes static electricity and can spark a fire or explosion. The humidity level is kept low at 40 percent to prevent bacterial growth, but this low level also increases the risk of static electricity. We check the humidity level and the temperature in each operating room every morning. The rooms are kept cool at sixty-eight to seventy-two degrees to prevent fluid from evaporating from the patients exposed tissues."

My mind began to wander as she was speaking. *I sweat easily. What if I get too hot wearing the cap, mask, and gown over my scrubs and sweat starts pouring down my forehead and dripping on the instrument table?* I decided to ask about it.

Miss Crowder responded with "That's a good question. The surgeons often perspire under the bright lights. If you start sweating, tell the circulating nurse. She'll blot your forehead with a towel. Just remember not to instinctively wipe off the sweat with your hand or sleeve."

After our tour and initial orientation, Miss Crowder left us with Mrs. Jones, head nurse in the operating room. We did not see our clinical instructor very often after that. Two days a week, we were in classes with Miss Brown, our medical-surgical instructor. Back to doing jumping jacks and learning about surgical nursing!

The surgical team included the surgeon, an anesthesiologist, a circulating nurse, and a scrub nurse. As student nurses, we took on the role of the scrub nurse under the supervision of the hospital's staff scrub nurse.

Mrs. Jones reviewed the duties of each nurse, saying, "The circulating nurse does what the title implies. She circulates around the operating room and adds needed supplies to the scrub nurse's tray. Now this is very important, so listen carefully. She will add more sponges to your tray. Each package should contain ten sponges. You are responsible for counting out loud the sponges dropped on your tray. This is crucial. When the surgery is finished, the wound can't be closed until the count is correct. A sponge is the most common surgical instrument left in patients.

"The scrub nurse stands with the surgeon and gives him the instruments and sponges at his request. There will be a large table at your side full of instruments and a smaller tray of instruments in front of you. The equipment the surgeon uses changes as the surgery progresses. The smaller tray is your working tray; it will have what is needed when the surgery begins. When different equipment is required, you will find it on the larger table to stock your tray. Tomorrow, you will spend the day observing surgeries."

In the afternoon after all the surgeries for the day were completed, the nurses cleaned the operating room. I helped them remove all the equipment stored in operating room cabinets and scrubbed the shelves with an antiseptic solution. The anesthesiologists did the final cleaning of their equipment, and housekeeping staff scrubbed the tables and floors. The rooms were spotless when we finished.

On Wednesday morning, I was assigned to operating room number 3 to observe a cholecystectomy (removal of gallbladder) in the morning and a vein ligation (tying the vein) and stripping in the afternoon. There was a large box of scrumptious-looking doughnuts sitting on the table in the operating room lounge. I was tempted to devour one before changing into my scrubs but resisted the urge. Maybe later. I changed into scrubs and put on shoe covers, a surgical cap, and a mask before going to the sink to scrub my hand for three minutes, the required time for an observer, before entering the operating room.

The number of instruments on the tables was breathtaking. I had never seen so many in one place and wondered how I could remember the names of all of them. Closer inspection revealed hemostats comprised the bulk of the instruments. The scrub nurse had prepared the instrument table using a list kept in Central Supply.

The scrub nurse said, "There's a sheet listing the equipment needed for each type of surgery, plus a list of glove sizes for each surgeon. I gathered everything listed and organized it all in accordance with sequence of use during the surgery. It takes time and experience to learn how to get the equipment arranged to keep the surgery moving along smoothly. Stand over here on this step stool so you get an unobstructed view."

The staff rolled the patient, Mrs. Heller, in on a stretcher and lifted her onto the narrow operating table. As soon she was positioned, the anesthesiologist started an IV and asked if Dr. Black, the surgeon, was ready.

The circulating nurse said, "He's scrubbing right now."

Dr. Black and his assistant, a hospital resident, walked in, and the anesthesiologist began administering anesthesia.

Dr. Black went through the procedure of getting gowned and gloved just as I had been taught. The circulating nurse removed Mrs. Heller's gown, and Dr. Black and his assistant placed sterile drapes over Mrs. Heller, leaving the operative site exposed. Using forceps, he picked up a gauze pad from a bowl of Betadine solution and scrubbed Mrs. Heller's belly, turning the skin orange.

He waited a few seconds for it to dry and then held out his hand without saying a word or looking up. The scrub nurse placed the scalpel handle firmly in the palm of his hand. He curled his fingers around the handle and moved his hand back over the patient. I wasn't sure I wanted to watch him make the incision and, for a split second, entertained the idea of not looking. He made a superficial incision, going through the skin only. It wasn't too gruesome to watch. Blood oozed out. The scrub nurse handed him a sponge, and he sopped up the blood. The sponge was made of a thick soft material. It was once white but now brown from bloodstains after many uses. Sponges were washed and resterilized after each surgery. He dropped the sponge in the circulating nurse's hand when he was finished. She placed it on the floor near the wall. Their movements were well choreographed.

Dr. Black placed the scalpel in a basin on the instrument table, explaining, "This blade is dirty after making the initial incision. I will use a different blade to cut through the fatty tissue and muscle."

Those were the first words spoken since the surgery started, and they were for my benefit. Dr. Black was teaching me. I was impressed.

Once the deeper incision was made, the scrub nurse handed retractors to the resident. They looked like small garden hoes. Using the retractors, the resident pulled the incision open. Dr. Black clamped off blood vessels with hemostats and cauterized small vessels. A large number of sponges were used to soak up the blood. It was difficult to see the sponges in the patient once they were saturated. They looked like part of the patient's tissue, and I understood how they could accidentally be left in a patient. As Dr. Black removed them, he gave them to the circulating nurse. She kept them neatly piled on the floor.

For my benefit, Dr. Black pointed to and named the various anatomical structures. I was mesmerized, watching, learning, and recalling what I had learned in my anatomy and physiology classes.

Before Dr. Black began closing the site, he probed around, looking for and removing sponges. The circulating nurse tallied up the number of sponges that she had placed in piles of ten, and the scrub nurse counted the remaining sponges on her table. The count was correct. Dr. Black proceeded to close the incision and had the resident suture the skin. When they finished, I walked out of the room and was surprised to see I had been mesmerized for two hours.

After removing my outer operating room garb, I went to the staff lounge and spotted the box of doughnuts. This time, I snatched a crème-filled doughnut with chocolate icing, plopped down on the sofa, and slowly ate the doughnut, savoring every bite. Watching my first surgery had not curbed my appetite.

Mrs. Jones found me and asked, "Well, what did you think after watching surgery?"

"I had imagined it was going to be all bloody and gory, but it wasn't like that at all. I liked it. It was entertaining, and I learned a lot."

"Would you like to see a T&A (tonsillectomy and adenoidectomy) before going to lunch?"

"Sure," I said.

"Dr. Hansen will be starting in about ten minutes in operating room number 4. It should take around fifty to sixty minutes from start to finish."

I scurried to get ready to watch the T&A. As I was scrubbing my hands, Dr. Hansen walked up to a sink. "Are you going to be watching me?" he asked as he turned on the water and picked up a brush.

"Yes."

"Good. I like having students in the room. This will be the third T&A I've done this morning, and I have one more to go after Bonnie. She is five years old and has had tonsillitis four times this year. It's time to get rid of them."

"You probably don't remember me, but you removed my tonsils about seven years ago," I said.

"What's your name?"

"Miss Swan, Nancy."

"Your name rings a bell."

"You took them out using local anesthesia."

"Oh, I remember. I don't do that very often."

We finished scrubbing and walked into the operating room. Bonnie was lying on the table, and the anesthesiologist was talking to her. She looked sleepy but had a sweet smile. *She won't be smiling when this is over,* I thought to myself, remembering when my tonsils were removed.

Dr. Hansen walked over to Bonnie and whispered something in her ear and then nodded his head, and the anesthesiologist started the anesthesia.

I wondered what he said and imagined he'd said something like, "You can have some ice cream when this is over," just as he'd told me years ago. It had sounded good, but I hadn't wanted any ice cream when he'd finished.

I stood by Dr. Hansen's side as he operated. He inserted a clamp to hold Bonnie's mouth open. First, he removed her adenoids, located in the upper part of her throat in the nasal passage. Once he pulled them out, he packed gauze in the area to soak up the blood. Next he cut the tonsil free; inserted a wire snare, which cut the tonsil loose; pulled it out; and packed the area with gauze, repeating the same procedure on her other tonsil. Bonnie's tonsils were large and covered with deep pockmarks from the multiple infections she had suffered.

Dr. Hansen said, "Normal tonsils are smaller and smooth. These look pretty nasty. She'll be glad they are gone."

He completed the surgery by removing the gauze packings and cauterizing the blood vessels. I smelled a faint slightly sweet odor of something burning. The whole procedure had taken forty minutes. It was much bloodier than I'd expected. I removed my mask and shoe covers, thanked Dr. Hansen for allowing me to observe, washed my hands, and walked to the cafeteria.

It was not my lucky day. They were serving liver and onions. I didn't want that after having watched the gallbladder removed from the underside of Mrs. Heller's liver. I decided to eat a hot dog.

After lunch, I prepared to observe the vein ligation and stripping on

Mrs. Jenkins, an assembly line worker. She had developed varicose veins after many years of standing on a concrete floor.

The sheet was removed to expose her legs. They looked like there were knotted, twisted ropes bulging under the skin surface from her groin to her ankle on both legs. To say they were ugly would be an understatement. I was appalled.

The surgeon, Dr. Spruill, made small incisions near her groin and knee and tied off the vein; using a long flexible metal vein stripper that looked like a thin metal tube with an acorn-shaped head, he fed the tube into the vein until it appeared through the lower incision. Dr. Spruill began pulling the stripper out at the knee incision. I could see the stripper with the bulging acorn top sliding down her leg under the skin pulling the vein and wrinkling it into a bundle below the acorn on the stripper. I cringed.

He repeated the procedure by making incisions just below Mrs. Jenkins' knee and at the ankle, pulled the vein out, and then proceeded to her other leg to do it all over again. When finished he applied small dressings over the incisions and wrapped both legs from groin to ankle with elastic bandages. Although I thought the surgery was interesting, I was glad it was over. The image of the veins being torn loose and dragged out was imprinted in my brain.

It was time for me to quit observing. I was the scrub nurse today. The instrument tables were set up in preparation for a hysterectomy and the removal of a mole on the patient's face. It was a common practice for surgeons to do a minor surgical procedure on patients after completing the main surgery. Mrs. Darden had asked her surgeon, Dr. Evans, to remove the mole while he had her asleep.

The staff scrub nurse, Mrs. Henson, showed me a set of French eye needles she had positioned on the table. "These will be used to suture the face because they leave less scarring than the regular closed eyed needles. Look at them closely. There is a slit where you can slide the suture on the needle."

I examined the needles and could barely see the slit.

The surgery went smoothly. I was grooving on being the scrub nurse. Dr. Evans had completed the hysterectomy and removed the mole. He was ready to suture Mrs. Darden's face.

"Give me the smallest needle you have," Dr. Evans said, unaware that I had a set of French eyes on my table.

I picked up the tiny needle and positioned it in the needle holder. The circulating nurse opened a packet of a very thin silk suture and dropped it on the table. I grasped the suture, tried repeatedly to slide it through the slit, and kept missing it. Dr. Evans was getting impatient. Without looking at me, he stretched out his hand and began snapping his fingers. Finally, it was threaded and ready. I slapped it in his hand.

He grasped the needle holder and moved his hand back into his line of vision. He hesitated, and then in slow motion, he drew it toward his eyes. His face grew redder and redder, and his eyes crossed.

Stopping just short of touching his face, he yelled, "Jesus Christ!" and threw it across the room.

I looked at Mrs. Henson. She shrugged her shoulders but didn't say a word. The circulating nurse walked across the room, seized the needle and holder, and placed them in the basin with the used scalpel. Maybe they were used to his tantrums.

After a few seconds of silence, Dr. Evans spoke to me in a little child's voice. "Please give me a thirteen millimeter curved needle with 6-0 silk."

I glanced over at the circulating nurse, who pointed to the needle on my tray. I was shaking but managed to thread the needle and hand it to him.

Glibly he said, "Thank you," and completed the surgery.

A week later, I spotted Dr. Evans in the surgical suite.

To my surprise, he walked over and sort of apologized by saying, "I don't know how you got that needle threaded."

"It was quite a feat, especially when you began snapping your fingers."

He laughed before wandering off.

Dr. Jackson, an orthopedic surgeon, walked into the operating room lounge singing, "Oh the weather outside is frightful," and jingling the change in his pocket. "I love all this ice and snow. It's a good day to make some money. I almost broke my leg getting here this morning." And he burst into a loud guffaw.

Dr. Jackson was at least six foot four and probably weighed close to three hundred pounds. His belly poked out the scrub top and it hung loosely at the bottom.

He looked at the box of doughnuts on the table and said, "I'll have one of those doughnuts with the mouse turds on top," and picked up a doughnut with brown sprinkles.

Today my assignment was different. Instead of being the scrub nurse, I was to sit in the operating room where Dr. Jackson was doing a spinal fusion and record the conversation for later analysis on how much of the conversation was patient centered.

Before the surgery commenced, the patient's leg had to be scrubbed for ten minutes in preparation for some bone to be removed for the fusion. I was asked to hold the patient's leg up off the operating table while the assistant surgeon, Dr. Bassett, scrubbed the leg with an antiseptic solution. Dr. Jackson was standing nearby waiting to get started. He would be working on the patient's back while Dr. Bassett was removing bone from the leg.

I was doing okay holding the patient's leg in the air for the first five minutes, but now the leg felt like it weighed a ton. I kept shifting my position, trying to find a way to hold my arms against my body to get some relief.

Dr. Jackson apparently knew holding a leg up was difficult and was watching me struggle.

He said, "Just stick his big toe in your belly button."

I was ready to sit down and begin recording the conversation after that ordeal. With aching arms I picked up my pen and notebook and took my place in a chair near the back wall of the operating room. The surgical team understood my assignment and took full advantage as they talked about nearly anything but the patient. I learned all the details of a party at Dr. Jackson's house on the previous Saturday and thought the recounting of events was embellished for my benefit. They provided nonstop talk that kept me writing frantically throughout the procedure and nearly drowned out the chilling chiseling sound of bone being taken from the patient's leg.

When the surgery was completed, Dr. Jackson asked, "Did you run out of ink?" as he passed by me and exited the room.

On November 22, 1963, I was scrub nurse for Dr. Horner, a vascular surgeon. He was performing a femoral popliteal bypass graft, a relatively new procedure, to establish blood flow to the patient's lower leg. I had been excited to have this assignment.

The evening prior to surgery, Dr. Horner asked me to meet with him and the patient in her hospital room. He had a Doppler stethoscope that could detect blood flow through the popliteal artery. After Dr. Horner examined the patient, he let me listen through the Doppler stethoscope for the sound of blood flowing through the artery. He carefully placed the stethoscope over the patient's artery and asked me to describe what I heard.

"I can't hear anything," I said

"That's right. You can't hear anything because there is no blood getting through the artery due to a complete blockage." He took the stethoscope and moved it to a different place on the patient's leg, handed the earpiece to me, and then asked, "Can you hear anything?"

"Yes. I hear a swooshing sound."

"Good. That is the sound of blood flowing through her femoral artery. I'm going to graft the femoral artery to the popliteal artery tomorrow to establish blood flow to her lower leg."

I sat quietly as he carefully explained the surgery to his patient and learned that he expected the surgery to take about four hours.

The next day, surgery had been in progress for nearly an hour when it was abruptly interrupted by a nurse opening the door to the operating room. She popped her head in the doorway and announced, "The president has been shot."

There was complete silence for a few seconds before Dr. Horner asked, "Do you know his condition?"

"The president's motorcade is rushing to a hospital. That's all I know. I'll go back and listen for more news."

That was the last of the news flashes. I stood scrubbed in for three additional long hours. During that time, the nurse's words echoed through my mind, and I surmised that no news was good news. Immediately after the patient was wheeled out, I tore off my outer garments and made a beeline to the lounge with the rest of the surgical team. Staff crowded around the TV; some were sobbing. I knew, before hearing the words, that President Kennedy was dead. I was stunned and stood in silence watching the news for a few minutes before returning to complete my work and getting ready to go home for the weekend.

With the rest of America, I spent the weekend glued to the TV. On Sunday, I was watching the accused assassinator, Lee Harvey Oswald, being transferred to another jail. A man jumped out from the crowd in front of him, and I heard a gunshot. It was surreal—a murder on live TV. The whole weekend was like a dream. On Monday morning, I was back at school for three days before leaving for Thanksgiving break.

After Thanksgiving break, I spent the next week working in the recovery room where I met two delightful nurses, Mrs. Lehman and Mrs. Kalas. When they weren't at a patient's bedside, they sat perched on high stools keeping an eye on the patients lined up in beds.

Blood pressure, pulse, and respirations were checked every fifteen minutes, and the dressing was inspected for signs of bleeding. I was assigned to care for two patients. As soon as one of my patients was taken to his or her room, I was given another patient. By the end of the day, I was in agony. The inside of my ears were rubbed raw from the stethoscope.

The next morning, I cringed when I placed the stethoscope earpiece in my ear.

Mrs. Lehman asked, "What's wrong?"

"My ears are killing me. They're excoriated inside."

"Let me see? Ouch, they look rough. I'll get some cotton balls and pad the earpiece." When she finished, she gingerly placed them in my ears.

"That helps. Thanks."

One of the male patients woke up. He lifted his head and spit on the floor. Mrs. Lehman sprinted to his bedside, handed him an emesis basin, and said," Spit in this." He put his head back on the pillow. She placed the basin beside his head, reiterated her instructions, and walked away. He lifted his head and spit more forcefully over the bed rail.

"I give up. Help me move his bed." We rolled his bed away from the other patients, and Mrs. Lehman said, "Go ahead. Spit all you want," which he did.

After working one week in the regular recovery room, I was sent to the day surgery recovery room for a week. Mrs. Barnes showed me the day surgery schedule while we were waiting for our first patient to arrive. Dr. Harding, my minister, was scheduled for a circumcision at ten in the morning.

"That's my minister," I blurted out without thinking.

"You'll get to know him a little better today," she said with a glint in her eyes and smiling.

I knew this was not going to turn out well. She was up to something. My only hope was that he wouldn't recognize me. When he arrived in the recovery room, I checked his vital signs and the surgical site.

Mrs. Barnes stopped by and nonchalantly wrapped a gauze strip around his penis, tied it in a big bow, and said, "I think he'll like his present."

Dr. Harding woke up and asked, "What?"

"Everything looks good," she said. I felt like kicking her.

I continued to check him every fifteen minutes. Once fully awake, he recognized me. I wanted to remove the bow, but was afraid he would wonder what I was doing.

An hour later, Mrs. Barnes said, "He can get ready to go home."

I gave him the good news and asked, "Who's going to drive you home?"

"My wife."

"While you're getting dressed, I'll ask her to move the car to the pickup area." I handed him his clothes, pulled the curtain around his bed, and found his wife in the waiting room. I returned with a wheelchair, wheeled him to his car, and went back to the recovery room.

The nurses were howling. I removed the sheets from his bed and threw away the gauze bow I found lying on the bed with his gown.

I worked the rest of the week in day surgery without any more embarrassing incidents. When the week was up, it was time for me to start a new rotation. I was going to miss surgery.

On Sunday morning, I went to church. As usual, I shook Dr. Harding's hand while leaving and thought about asking if he was doing okay. Fortunately, he didn't mention the surgery. Neither did I.

BACK TO MEDICAL-SURGICAL NURSING

In December 1963, I began my final six-month stint, consisting of medical-surgical nursing and classroom courses. My rotation was on one of the wards in the new six-story addition that was completed in mid-1963. All patient rooms were private or semiprivate. Thankfully, there were no six-bed wards! Every room had a bathroom, shower, wall suction, and piped-in oxygen. The toilets had arms that swung down over the bowl for spraying and cleaning bedpans. I loved the thought of having modern equipment.

The first day back, I was assigned to work with two patients—Mr. Singer, a prominent businessman who had an inguinal hernia repair the previous day, and Mr. Bradley, who'd suffered a stroke eight days earlier. *This should be an easy assignment,* I thought. *Mr. Singer won't take much time. I'll be able to give Mr. Bradley the attention he needs.*

The nursing supervisor, Mrs. Nesbitt, was chatting with Mr. Singer when I entered his room carrying a stethoscope, blood pressure cuff, and thermometer, eager to get started. My presence was totally ignored. The longer I waited, the antsier and more annoyed I became. After waiting five minutes for them to finish their conversation, I was finally able to check Mr. Singer's vital signs and his dressing and bring him his breakfast tray.

"I want to sit on the side of the bed," he said.

"Okay."

He sat up without assistance and dangled his legs over the side of the bed.

"Do you have everything you need?"

He began rearranging the things on his tray and nodded.

"I'll be back in about twenty minutes," I said and left to check in on Mr. Bradley.

Mr. Bradley was slouched over and scrunched up in the middle of the bed. His left eyelid and the left corner of his mouth drooped. He moved his lips in an attempt to speak. No words came out. Gluey strands of saliva stretched between his sticky lips. I pulled him up in the bed, checked his vital signs, and cleaned his mouth with a lemon glycerin swab before giving him his tray of pureed food and placing a spoon in his right hand. He dropped it. I picked it up and fed him. Before leaving his room, I positioned him on his side, propped him with some pillows, and placed the call bell near his left hand. Thirty minutes had passed.

"Where have you been? " Mr. Singer inquired. "You said you would be back in twenty minutes."

"I was helping another patient. It took longer than I anticipated."

"I'm ready to get up and get a shower."

"You can't shower until your doctor gives approval."

"I'm going to get a shower." He sat up and started to get out of bed.

"Let me check with the head nurse."

I returned with bad news. "The head nurse said you can't take a shower today. You'll have to wait until Dr. Franklin removes the dressing and writes an order for a shower."

"That's ridiculous. Why do you have showers if we can't use them?"

Thinking that this was a rhetorical question, I remained silent. Once his bath supplies were ready, I pulled the curtain around his bed and said, "I'll be back in about ten minutes."

When I returned to Mr. Singer's room, the washcloth had not been touched.

"What's the matter?"

"I hurt too bad. You need to help me." He groaned and flaunted a smug smile.

"You can have some pain medicine and rest before you bathe."

"I don't want or need pain medicine. You need to help me."

I thought about Mr. Bradley, who was in real need of help. But instead of displaying my fury, I refilled the basin with fresh hot water and handed the washcloth to him.

He refused to take it, saying, "It hurts to move."

I gave up and hurriedly bathed Mr. Singer as he lay limp and helpless. I finished and scurried back to Mr. Bradley's room. As soon as I got his bath supplies ready, an announcement came over the intercom. "Miss Swan, please come to the nursing station."

Mrs. Nesbitt was waiting for me. "Mr. Singer called me. He said you didn't wash his feet."

I felt like telling her to go wash his feet while I cared for Mr. Bradley. Mrs. Nesbitt wasn't stupid. She chose to encourage Mr. Singer's manipulative behavior. Instead, I trotted back to his room and said, "I'm sorry I forgot to wash your feet."

He looked squarely in my eyes without uttering a word. In silence, I gathered the equipment again. Mr. Singer didn't use one muscle to help lift his leg for me to place his foot in the basin of water. As soon as I let go, his leg began to topple over. I caught it in the nick of time, preventing the basin from tipping and spilling water all over the freshly made bed. When I finished and started to exit the room, Mr. Singer said, "Bring me some 7 Up."

I fetched the 7 Up and then returned to Mr. Bradley's room to give him his morning care. I was proud when finished. Mr. Bradley looked comfortable and 200 percent better.

The next morning, the head nurse laughed nervously. "I've changed your assignment. Mr. Singer said he didn't want a student nurse. He requested someone who knew what she was doing. I gave you Mrs. Padgett. She had a hysterectomy a week ago."

"I knew he was none too pleased with me."

"Don't worry about it. We'll deal with him."

About midmorning, I was walking down the hall and passed Mr. Singer standing in the doorway of his room. "Good morning, Mr. Singer."

He stared straight through me without uttering a sound.

My day went smoothly. I spent quality time with Mr. Bradley and fully appreciated Mrs. Padgett's sweet disposition.

Permeating the ward was a foul, sickening smell. Immediately I knew it was the odor of bloody stools. There was no other smell in the world like it. Mr. Ingle was my assigned patient. He had a bleeding ulcer. I sat down for morning report and asked the night nurse, "Is that smell coming from Mr. Ingle's room?"

"Yes. I'll tell you about him when I give report."

Everyone was present, and the shift report was in progress. "Mr. Ingle is a forty-eight-year-old white male admitted yesterday with a bleeding peptic ulcer. He had a large, black, tarry stool this morning that I'm sure everyone smelled. His vital signs are stable. He's on complete bed rest, NPO [nothing by mouth], vital signs every thirty minutes, and receiving the third unit of blood. There are four more units on standby. Lab is to do a stat hematocrit and hemoglobin level when this unit is finished, and Dr. Young is to be notified of the results. Keep the vein open with D5W [5 percent dextrose in water] between transfusions. He's scheduled at 11:00 a.m. for a subtotal gastrectomy and a vagotomy." The first procedure would entail the removal of the lower two-thirds of the stomach, and the second would sever his vagus nerve to decrease production of acid in the stomach.

While I tended him, Mr. Ingle said, "I'll be glad to get this surgery over with. For the past year and a half, I've been in constant pain. Nothing has worked. I've tried every antacid on the market and stuck to my diet. I've avoided spicy and fatty foods, raw fruits and vegetables, and even given up drinking coffee. It was hardly worth eating. This is my last hope. Dr. Young is going to check my blood later. He thinks after I get this blood, I'll be ready for surgery."

"He put you on the schedule for 11:00 a.m. Did he explain the surgery?"

"He's going to remove the lower part of my stomach and cut the nerve that causes acid production. He called it a surgical antacid. If everything goes smoothly, I'll go home in two weeks."

"Are you having any pain?"

"Yes. The only time I don't have pain is after I eat, but two to three hours later, the pain is back. It's a burning pain right here," he said, pointing to the upper part of his abdomen.

His lab work came back, and Dr. Young was notified. Mr. Ingram was stable for surgery. I helped him bathe, shaved and scrubbed his abdomen with an antibacterial soap, and gave him his preop medications. After he was taken to surgery, I prepared the room for his return. He was not back from the recovery room by the time I left for the day.

In the morning, I greeted him with "It's good to see you. How was your night?"

"I've been having pain, but it's different. It's from the surgery. The nurse kept me as comfortable as she could."

He had an IV, a nasogastric tube connected to suction, urinary catheter, and a tube protruding from his abdomen and connected to a drainage bottle. The surgeon had removed the lower two-thirds of Mr. Ingle's stomach and the first portion of his small intestine (duodenum). The remaining portion of his stomach was connected to the jejunum (second part of the small intestine). This is the same procedure used today in gastric bypass surgery for weight loss.

"I'll be able to start eating once my doctor hears bowel sounds. He said that could take a day or two."

The next morning, he said, "I'm starting to get hungry. Maybe I'll get to eat."

"That's a good sign. You'll have to take it easy though. Your stomach is a lot smaller than it was. It will take time to get adjusted."

"What do you mean?"

"You won't be able to eat much, and the food will quickly empty into your intestines. Diarrhea is common at first."

Mr. Ingle was right. The surgeon heard bowel sounds and ordered a clear liquid diet. I clamped the nasogastric tube and gave him some Jell-O.

"This tastes divine. I never thought I'd say that about Jell-O."

"Just remember to eat slowly."

"Okay." He finished the bowl of Jell-O. "I think that's enough for now."

He sipped on water and juice throughout the morning.

"This is going better than I thought it would. I haven't had any pain or diarrhea."

The next morning, Dr. Young ordered removal of the nasogastric tube and a full liquid diet and discontinued intravenous fluids. Mr. Ingle's breakfast consisted of juice and custard, which he tolerated.

Mr. Ingle was discharged sixteen days after his surgery.

Three months later, I learned that Mr. Ingle was back in the hospital.

He had begun experiencing symptoms of dumping syndrome. As the remaining portion of his stomach was stretched, the food in his stomach was suddenly dumped into his jejunum, causing sweating, faintness, and nausea. The carbohydrates in his jejunum were rapidly absorbed, leading to an overproduction of insulin with a drop in blood sugar. He had to be admitted to get him on the right diet in order to gain some weight. He was malnourished and had lost eighteen ponds. Mr. Ingle was put on a low-carbohydrate, high-protein diet. Small portions were served six to eight times a day. Mr. Ingle was reluctant to eat anything at first and needed help understanding what was happening and how these foods and frequent feedings would help. Once he understood, he was willing to try. Five days later, he was discharged and doing much better.

Most of the patients on the ward were there for heart attacks, congestive heart failure, fractures, strokes, high blood pressure, pneumonia, cancer, and kidney stones. The common surgeries included appendectomies, cholecystectomies, hysterectomies, hernia repairs, and hemorrhoidectomies. I was getting proficient at caring for patients with these problems. Even though I liked having the opportunity to care for patients with common problems, I appreciated it when I had a chance to work with a patient with an illness or disease I had not seen. Mrs. Cahill fit the bill.

She had been admitted to the unit the previous evening with a detached retina. Her orders included strict bed rest, lying flat on her back, and keeping both eyes patched.

I made a little noise as I walked into her room so I would not startle her. She was middle-aged. A pink mesh net covered her salt-and-pepper hair, and white gauze patches covered both eyes. Above her left eye was a black X made with a marker. It indicated the eye with the detached retina.

"Good morning, Mrs. Cahill. My name is Miss Swan. How are you this morning?"

"I guess I'm doing all right. What did you say your name was?"

"Miss Swan. I'm a student nurse. I'll be taking care of you this morning."

"It's nice to meet you, honey. I've been awake all night. I can't see. I can't do anything. I'm not allowed to turn on my side or have a pillow. This is awful. I'm thirsty, but I don't know where my water is."

"It is here on your bedside table. I'll pour a glass of fresh cold water for you."

"That would be nice."

I was thinking about her calling me honey. I had called my boyfriend honey one time, and he told me I had the wrong person, saying he was sweetie. I almost chuckled out loud thinking about that, but I held the glass of fresh water steady and touched her lips with the straw. She guzzled it to the last drop.

"That was good. Thanks, honey."

"You're welcome. Before I get your breakfast tray, I'm going to check your blood pressure and temperature. I'll tell you each thing I'm going to do. No surprises."

I picked up the blood pressure cuff and put it on her arm as I described the procedure. "I'm going to put the stethoscope on your arm. It may feel cold." As I was checking her vital signs, the dietary staff brought her breakfast tray. "You're breakfast smells good. Can you smell it?"

"Bacon and coffee," she said, smiling.

I took the cover off the plate. "You're good. There's bacon, scrambled eggs, coffee, orange juice, milk, toast, and jelly. I'll feed it to you. Don't lift your head up or turn it. What would you like first?"

"I believe I'll start with the juice." When she finished eating everything on her plate, she said, "That was so nice of you, honey. I hate to be such a bother."

"You certainly are not a bother."

"I have a question. Why are both of my eyes covered?"

"So you won't be looking around. The eyes work together. If you move your right eye, your left eye will move too. It has to be kept still. When did you notice that something was wrong with your eye?"

"A couple days ago. I thought there was a hair in it. I looked and couldn't find a hair. Later that day, I started seeing flashes of light. I decided I would make an appointment to see my eye doctor. The next morning, I called Dr. Rose's office." Dr. Rose was an ophthalmologist. "I was told to come in right away. By the time I got to his office, I couldn't see out of part of my eye. It was like someone was pulling a curtain over it. He took one look and said I had a detached retina and sent me straight to the hospital. Honey, that scared me."

"It would have scared me, too."

"Am I going to be blind in that eye?"

"It's going to take some time for your sight to come back. Your doctor has you flat on your back in hopes that your retina will reattach itself."

Dr. Rose checked Mrs. Cahill's eye later that morning. "Can you see anything with your left eye?" he asked.

"No, nothing. It's pitch-black."

"I can take you to the operating room tomorrow morning and do surgery. If I don't do surgery, you will need to lie completely still for at least four months. Even after all that time, you may not regain your sight. There's a new procedure that we've been doing for about a year where I can put a band around your eye to hold your retina in place. You will be able to get out of bed in three days."

"Will I be able to see?"

"It will take time. The retina needs to reattach itself. The band helps speed up the process."

"Will I have to go back to surgery to have the band removed?"

"No. It will stay in your eye permanently."

"Will the band block part of my sight?"

"No. It isn't put over the front of your eye. You won't know it's there."

"How many times have you done this kind of surgery?"

"I don't know. I've lost count."

I was fascinated with Mrs. Cahill's questions. She had an inquisitive mind and was able to think clearly while under stress. I had been with patients who never questioned their doctors.

Mrs. Cahill decided to have surgery. Dr. Rose got her on the operating room schedule and wrote preoperative orders.

After he left her room, Mrs. Cahill said. "Oh, honey, I hope this works."

"Dr. Rose sounded confident."

Secretly, I was wondering how many of these surgeries he had actually done. I had not seen any, but I had been doing my specialty rotations for the past year. He had said it was a new procedure. I wanted to find more information. All I learned was that the procedure was called scleral buckling. It was too early to determine the success rates.

Mrs. Cahill had her surgery the following morning.

Dr. Rose came to check on her after lunch and told her, "The surgery went well. You had a tear in your eye that caused fluid to leak out and detach the retina. I drained the fluid and patched the tear before I put the band around your eye. Everything went smoothly."

"I'm having some pain in my eye. Is that normal?"

"Yes. I've ordered some pain medicine for you. Just ask the nurse if you need something. Would you like some now?"

"That would be nice."

I gave Mrs. Cahill her pain medicine. She spent most of the afternoon resting. Mrs. Cahill was discharged from the hospital five days after her surgery.

I saw Dr. Rose about a month later and asked how she was doing.

"She is slowly regaining her sight in that eye. Right now, it is blurry. I think she will regain full vision."

"That's good to hear. A year ago, I wouldn't have expected her to get her sight back."

Dr. Rose smiled. "You're right. Things are constantly changing for the better."

A large man was lying in a hospital bed in front of the nursing station. It wasn't unusual to see a patient in bed in the hall, but it was unusual to see the bed placed directly in front of the nursing station. Immediately, I knew his condition was unstable, and the nurses were watching him closely. I paused to look at him before walking into the nursing station. He looked vaguely familiar.

"Who is that man in the hall?"

"Mr. Lamb."

"I thought I recognized him. I took care of his granddaughter last year in pediatrics. She was diagnosed with cystic fibrosis. He was devastated."

I followed the night nurse down the hall to the report room. Mr. Lamb was fifty-six years old and had been diagnosed with diabetes mellitus when he was twelve years old. He was overweight and had high blood pressure, heart disease, and poor circulation. Mr. Lamb had injured his lower leg, and the wound would not heal. Infection had set in and then gangrene, and it had become necessary to amputate his leg. During the night, his condition began deteriorating—his blood pressure fell steadily, his pulse increased, his respirations grew shallow, and he experienced a decreased level of consciousness. The nursing staff moved him near the nursing station and called Dr. Young, his surgeon.

A few minutes later, Dr. Young arrived. I stood nearby and watched as he examined Mr. Lamb. Suddenly, Dr. Young hopped up in the bed, straddled his legs over Mr. Lamb, and began pushing down repeatedly on Mr. Lamb's chest. More staff began gathering around the bed to get a closer look. I was wondering what on earth he was doing.

About a minute passed before he stopped and felt Mr. Lamb's neck. I assumed he was checking for a pulse. He resumed pushing.

This went on for some time, maybe ten minutes, before Dr. Hayes climbed off the bed, placed his stethoscope over Mr. Lamb's heart, and said, "His heart stopped, and I can't get it restarted." He pulled the sheet over his body and pronounced him dead at 7:56 a.m. "I was compressing his heart and hoping it would start beating on its own again," he added. "I read about how to do this in the journal last night."

I was excited and couldn't wait for my shift to end so I could tell my classmates what I had witnessed. This was the beginning of cardiopulmonary resuscitation, and little did I know, it would change the delivery of care for critically ill patients. It wasn't long before coronary care units began opening in hospitals across the country, and lives were being saved as the technology improved.

In the last three months of nursing school, we worked three days a week on the medical surgical units with full patient assignments to prepare us for the real world of nursing. Mrs. Hankins was an attractive young adult with the largest goiter I had ever seen bulging out on the right side of her neck. It was hard for me not to stare at it. The Great Lakes region was known as the goiter belt because the soil lacked iodine. I had seen plenty of goiters but never one the size of a grapefruit. My mother always bought iodized salt, which was first sold in grocery stores in 1924 when my mother was eleven years old. She taught me to never buy any other type of salt, saying it prevented goiters. I wondered why there were still so many people with goiters. In nursing school, I learned there were other conditions that caused an enlarged thyroid gland.

The thyroid gland, located in the neck, is made up of two lobes and an isthmus that lies over the trachea and joins the lobes. Mrs. Hankins had a single large nodule in the right lobe of her thyroid pressing on her esophagus and trachea. She was scheduled to have the right lobe and isthmus removed (subtotal thyroidectomy).

I introduced myself to Mrs. Hankins and told her I would be getting her ready for surgery. "Do you have any questions?"

"No. I'm starting to get nervous. I've never had surgery."

"What are your concerns?"

"I'm afraid I'll die."

"Have you talked with your surgeon about that?"

"No, but I've been thinking about it since he explained the surgery. He said death could be a complication."

"Doctors have to tell you every possible thing that could go wrong. Dying in surgery is very rare."

"My aunt told me she knew of someone who died."

"That's not a problem in this day and time. Medicine has come a long way in the past few years, and doctors know which medicines to give before surgery to prevent complications. Patients who had hyperthyroidism were at risk during surgery. You do not have hyperthyroidism, which is an overactive thyroid gland."

"That's good to hear. I'll be glad to get rid of this goiter. It's getting hard for me to swallow, and I get short of breath just walking. I'll look better too. I've heard children asking their moms what was wrong with me and mothers telling their children to shush. I felt ugly and embarrassed. I want the surgery, and I don't want it. You must think I'm a basket case."

"I think you know what you want, but you're scared."

"Yeah. It's going to be a long night waiting for surgery."

"Around nine o'clock this evening, I'll give you a sleeping pill and a back rub to help you relax and get some sleep. Before I do that, I will need to give you some enemas."

"Why?"

"Anesthesia and pain medications slow everything down. You will be more comfortable after surgery if you aren't constipated and straining to have a stool."

"That makes sense. I had to get an enema before my children were born. It was uncomfortable but not too bad."

By the time I left the unit for the night, Mrs. Hankins was fast asleep and snoring loudly. Her roommate was complaining about the snoring. I gave her some cotton balls to plug her ears and told her the snoring should stop after Mrs. Hankins's surgery.

The next evening, I found Mrs. Hankins resting in a semisitting position in her bed. She had a large dressing covering her neck. I softly called her name, and she opened her eyes.

"Hi. It's good to see you. I need to check your blood pressure and your dressing."

I felt behind her neck and shoulders to make sure no blood was running down under her. "Are you having any trouble breathing?"

"No."

Her voice was hoarse, most likely from swelling in her throat and having had a tube in her throat during surgery. If she had symptoms of laryngeal obstruction, she would need a tracheostomy. I had checked to make sure there was a tracheostomy tray available on the unit. There was one on the countertop in the clean utility room.

Mrs. Hankins's evening was uneventful. I kept her comfortable and checked on her frequently.

It was shortly after ten o'clock in the evening when I head a call bell ring. It was my patient, Mr. Hartley. He was in the hospital with congestive heart failure. Mr. Hartley was only fifty-three-years-old and had a history of two heart attacks—one at the age of forty-nine and the second one three months earlier.

I walked down the long, dimly lit hall to Mr. Hartley's room. As soon as I'd entered his room, he gasped and said, "I can't breathe."

He had a wild look in his eyes and was struggling to sit up in the bed. A shiver ran down my spine.

"Let me help you. I'll crank up the head of your bed."

Trying to look calm yet sensing the urgency of the situation, I turned off his call light and pulled it again to get the attention of staff in the nursing station. Mr. Hartley grabbed my arm and began pleading for me to help him get out of bed. He tugged on my arm trying to get up, but he was too weak.

"I've called for the nurse. You need to lie still. Moving around will make it harder to breathe."

"Let me get up. I can't breathe," he gasped while still attempting to get out of bed.

The nurse, Mrs. Parks, arrived, took one look at Mr. Hartley, and said,

"Start oxygen at six liters per minute." Pivoting around quickly to exit the room, she said, "I'm going to call the resident."

I turned on the oxygen and grabbed the tubing and cannula hanging from the piped-in oxygen outlet. Mr. Hartley flailed his arms about, preventing me from getting the cannula in his nose.

"Mr. Hartley, I need put this in your nose. It will help you breathe."

"I have to get up."

He began hitting my arms and looked like a trapped wild animal fighting for its life.

Suddenly, his breathing changed from gasping to gurgling sounds, and he quit fighting. I poked the cannula prongs in his nose and silently prayed for the staff to get in here.

Mrs. Parks ran into the room with a blood pressure cuff and stethoscope swinging in her hand. She had just started to wrap the cuff around Mr. Hartley's arm when the medical resident, Dr. Gymoti, walked in.

He grabbed the stethoscope from Mrs. Parks and listened to Mr. Hartley's chest. Mr. Hartley coughed up some frothy-bloody sputum.

Dr. Gymoti looked directly at me and commanded, "Get three tourniquets!"

My thoughts were racing as I rushed out of the room. Rotating tourniquets were used to treat acute pulmonary edema, a collection of fluid in the air sacs of the lungs caused by failure of the heart to pump blood out to the body. Tourniquets were used to decrease the amount of blood returning to the heart by placing them on three extremities at a time and rotating them every fifteen minutes. I was planning what to do once I got back to Mr. Hartley's room.

I hustled back to his room clutching the rubber tourniquets. Dr. Gymoti snatched them out of my hand and put them on Mr. Hartley. The gurgling sounds ceased. I sighed a breath of relief but then noticed Mr. Hartley had stopped breathing. His body was limp and pale; his jaw hung open. I stood there stunned, watching Dr. Gymoti remove the tourniquets and pull the sheet up over his face.

The next day, back in the dormitory, I recounted the experience with my peers. We talked about our feelings, our limitations, and our own mortality. In an effort to relieve some of our stress, we played a practical joke on our classmates. We found some Saran wrap and spread it tightly across the rims of the toilet bowls in the dormitory bathroom. Then we sat in a room near the bathroom, talking and waiting for a victim. I had gotten

so involved in our conversation I almost forgot about our little prank until I heard a scream. Simultaneously, we broke out in laughter. It felt good.

The next evening, I was relaxed and ready for my new assignment. Around suppertime, my instructor asked me to admit fifty-eight-year-old Mr. Crozier, sent to the unit from the emergency room.

Mr. Crozier had gone to work that morning feeling his normal self. He was a healthy, active male who enjoyed playing basketball with his grandchildren, went golfing on weekends, and had no history of medical problems.

He said, "By two o'clock, I could only take a few steps at a time without having to stop and rest. I went to the bathroom but was too weak to open the door and called for help. My boss summoned an ambulance, and that is how I got here."

I was intrigued by his story and didn't have a clue about what was happening to him. Neither did his doctor. The admission diagnosis was extreme weakness.

"Your doctor wants you to stay in bed and rest for now. He ordered some lab work and will see you in the morning. Call me if you need anything. Don't try to get out of bed."

Each time I checked on Mr. Crozier, he reported feeling fine. By the time my shift was over, Mr. Crozier was sleeping peacefully.

When I arrived on the unit the following evening, my thoughts turned to Mr. Crozier. I wondered if the doctor had made a diagnosis. The nurse finished giving report, and Mr. Crozier's name never came up. I asked, "Where's Mr. Crozier?"

"He died."

"What?" I was caught off guard.

"We thought he was doing well. He began having trouble breathing, and within thirty minutes, he died. His doctor is taking it the hardest. He reviewed all Mr. Crozier's symptoms and thinks he missed a diagnosis of myasthenia gravis. The rapid progression of symptoms was not typical. He said if he had known, he would have started neostigmine injections, which most likely would have saved his life."

Myasthenia gravis is an autoimmune disease when the body, for some unknown reason, produces antibodies against the neurotransmitter acetylcholine. Acetylcholine is needed for nerve impulses to stimulate muscles. Neostigmine improves muscle function by slowing down the breakdown of acetylcholine, making more of it available for nerve stimulation. Patients with myasthenia gravis are maintained on this drug for the remainder of their lives. Since the drug is short acting, it must be taken every four hours around the clock. If patients keep up with this regimen, they have a normal life expectancy.

I had to move on and take care of my patients, even though I felt like being alone to grieve. Mrs. Norris had a bowel obstruction and was scheduled for an exploratory laparotomy in the morning to learn the cause of the obstruction. Dr. Franklin, her surgeon, had discussed the possibility of returning from surgery with a colostomy.

After giving her soapsuds enemas until the results returned clear, I would need to scrub and shave her abdomen, being careful not to make any nicks to prevent any potential sites for infection. I collected a metal enema bucket with tubing and a clamp, an IV pole, packets of castile soap, K-Y jelly, a thermometer, and a bed pad. After assembling the equipment at Mrs. Norris's bedside, I poured a packet of the castile soap into the enema bucket, filled the bucket with 1,500 milliliters (one and a half quarts) of water at 105 degrees Fahrenheit, and hung the bucket on the IV pole.

Mrs. Norris rolled over on her left side, and I began administering the enema. Almost immediately, Mrs. Norris complained of cramping, saying, "I can't hold it."

"Take some deep breaths. I'll slow it down."

She took deep breaths, groaned, and complained, but before long, most of the solution in the bucket was gone. She began expelling some of the water. I clamped the tube and pushed the bedpan under her, saying, "Hold it in as long as you can."

Ten minutes later, I peeked behind her curtain and asked, "How are you doing?"

"I'm finished, I think."

"Okay. Let's see the results. The water isn't clear. I'll need to give you another enema."

"Really?"

"Yes. Maybe this will be the last one."

The second time, when I took her off the bedpan, I spotted a tennis ball-size clump of squiggly worms wound tightly together.

"Is it clear this time?" she asked.

Scrambling to find an answer without lying or looking shocked, I said, "I'll have my instructor take a look and see what she thinks." I covered the bedpan and placed it in the bathroom before searching for Miss Polsky.

When I found her, I said, "You have to see what I found in the enema results on Mrs. Morgan."

"What did you find?"

"A ball of worms."

She followed me to the patient's room. I watched as she peered at the contents. She stared, mouth gaping at the discovery, and then whispered, "Cover the bedpan and take it to the dirty utility room."

Once we got there she said, "Those look like roundworms. We need to save them for pathology. Find a sterile specimen bottle."

I saw one of my classmates as I walked down the hall and stopped to tell her what happened. The word spread rapidly, and there was a steady stream of staff to and from the utility room and a lot of oohing and ahhing.

The head nurse called Dr. Franklin. He canceled the surgery and instructed her to send the worms to the pathology department for identification. He would decide what to do once he saw the pathology report.

I asked Miss Polsky what I should tell Mrs. Norris.

"Tell her the surgery has been canceled. We think she passed what was causing the obstruction."

When I arrived, the first thing she asked was "Do I have to have another enema?"

"No. I have good news for you. Your surgery has been canceled. We think the enema cleared the obstruction."

"What? I'm speechless." She paused before continuing, "Thank you. Can I go home?"

"Not yet. Dr. Franklin wants to see the pathology results first."

The next evening, Dr. Franklin entered Mrs. Norris's room bearing a big smile. "I just came from the lab. You passed a ball of roundworms last night. I'm—"

Mrs. Norris interrupted him. "What did you say?"

"You had worms. That's what caused the obstruction. The enemas washed them out. I'm going to order some medicine that will kill any eggs that may be left behind."

She looked pale. "What did they look like?"

"They were wound together in a ball."

"How did I get them?"

"Have you traveled out of the country?"

"No."

"So we can rule that out. Do you eat fresh fruits and vegetables?"

"Yes."

"You must have gotten some that were contaminated."

"What does that mean?"

"Vegetables and fruits that were grown in contaminated soil that contained the eggs from worms. They're too small to be seen without a microscope. That's why it's important to scrub them first if you are going to eat them raw."

"That's gross. I don't think I'll eat raw fruits and vegetables again."

"You don't have to give them up. Just scrub them real good before you eat them. I'll order some medicine and get it started this evening. You should be able to go home tomorrow."

After supper, I administered the first dose of the antihelmintic (a type of drug used to get rid of worms) to Mrs. Norris. "The name of this medicine is Delvex. It will cause your stools to turn blue. You will be taking it three times a day after you eat for five days. Make sure to swallow the tablet whole. Never chew or break it."

"Why can't I break it? I have a hard time swallowing pills?"

"The pills have a special coating on them so they won't dissolve until they get past the stomach. If you break them, they'll dissolve in the stomach and could cause nausea, vomiting, and diarrhea."

"Okay. Give it to me. I'll try to swallow it whole."

After a couple attempts, she was able to get the pill down.

Mrs. Norris was a thin woman. "Have you always been slender?" I asked.

"No. I've lost over thirty pounds in the past few months without trying. I guess it was the worms. Over the years, I tried dieting many times and was so glad when I finally lost some weight. I never questioned why."

My mind wandered back to a time when I was in high school. My best friend's mother was overweight and had bought some diet pills. I recalled her telling me, "I sat the bag with the pills by the hot radiator and forgot about them. A few hours later, I got the box of pills and opened it up. The capsules had melted, and there were worms crawling out of them."

I had been grossed out. She'd stood there laughing at me. When she'd finished laughing, she said, "I threw them away. I'd rather be fat." And she'd laughed again.

After regaining my composure, I'd asked, "Did that really happen?"

"That's the truth," she had insisted.

Miss Polsky asked me to do a presentation on ascariasis, an infestation of roundworms in the human body, for post conference the next day. I spent time in the school library looking up everything I could find about ascariasis. By the time I returned to the hospital, I was ready for my presentation.

My presentation went well. My classmates were unhinged by the details. I took great pleasure in watching their responses when I told them how the eggs are ingested and hatch larvae in the intestines. The larvae work their way through the intestinal wall and get in the bloodstream or lymphatic system and travel to the lungs where they mature into small roundworms. Once mature, they are coughed out of the lungs into the airway and travel up the throat or are swallowed. Some people discover they have worms when they sneeze a twelve- to fourteen-inch long worm out their nose.

Graduation was just around the corner. It was my last week working the evening shift on the medical-surgical unit.

The next afternoon, as I was fastening the studs on the bib to my apron, I thought about having only two more days to wear my student nurse uniform. I carefully pulled the bib over my shoulders and fastened the apron around my waist and looked at myself in the mirror, thinking about all I had experienced since the first time I had worn my student nurse uniform. My mind was flooded with memories of joys, sorrows, fears, and anxieties.

I picked up my cap with the three black velvet stripes and remembered my thrill at receiving each stripe. It seemed ironic that, in just a few days, I would be even more thrilled to remove the stripes and wear an all-white cap.

When my classmates and I walked into the report room on our last night, the staff cheered and had soft drinks and snacks for us. Before we left the ward for the last time as student nurses, we shared hugs and tears.

Walking back to the dorm I shouted, "We did it."

PROFESSIONAL NURSING

Is nursing a profession? This question, which I had been hearing for nearly three years, was finally going to be answered in our course on professional nursing, or so I thought. Mrs. Davis, director of our nursing school and an exemplary role model for nursing, taught the course during our final three months. There was a faction who argued nursing diploma programs (hospital based three-year programs) were an apprenticeship. They postulated that, for nursing to be a profession, entry into a nursing program needed to be at the baccalaureate level in a university setting. Students would receive a more rounded education and learn concepts and theories, rather than skills. Another group was proposing two levels of nursing—a technical nurse, who would be educated in a two-year program at a junior college, and a professional nurse, who would attend a four-year program. Both factions were advocating to get nurses' training out of hospital-based programs.

We began by learning about nurse innovators who, through the years, had elevated the standards of nursing. A brief list of some of these nurses included Florence Nightingale, Linda Richards, Lillian D. Wald, and Mary Mahoney.

Florence Nightingale is called the founder of modern nursing. Although born in 1820 in Florence, Italy, to an affluent family who considered nursing to be a lowly, menial job, Florence felt called to be a nurse. At age twenty-four, defying her mother's wishes, she enrolled in a training program at the Lutheran Hospital of Pastor Fliedner in Kaiserswerth, Germany. After completing her training in three months, she worked in London hospitals and, in 1853, became superintendent at the Hospital for Invalid Gentlewomen. Believing that dirt, not germs caused disease, she improved the hospital's sanitary conditions and dramatically reduced the death rate.

The British Secretary of War, a personal friend who heard of her accomplishments, asked her to organize a corps of nurses to care for hospitalized British soldiers in Crimea. Female nurses had never been used in the military. Miss Nightingale recruited nearly forty nurses to go with her to the British base.

The hospital was disgraceful. More soldiers were dying from infectious diseases than from battle injuries. She recruited able-bodied patients to scrub the inside of the hospital from floor to ceiling, while she spent her time caring for the soldiers. After dark, she carried a lamp while ministering to the patients and writing letters for them. The soldiers were so moved by her compassion that they began calling her the "Lady with the Lamp" and kissed her shadow as she passed by. Once again, her work reduced the death rate significantly.

Additional accomplishments while she was there included establishing a kitchen for preparing special diets, setting up a hospital laundry, and creating a classroom and library for the patients.

After the war, Miss Nightingale received a hero's welcome home and was granted $250,000 from the British government. She used the money to fund the Nightingale Training School for Nurses at St. Thomas Hospital in London, the first scientifically based nursing program. Young women, including those from the upper class, began enrolling in the program.

Linda Richards, America's first trained nurse, graduated from the New England Hospital for Women and Children in 1873. She introduced the practice of keeping patient records, doctor's orders, and nurse's notes and wearing uniforms.

Lillian D. Wald graduated from the New York Hospital Training School for Nurses and worked in New York's lower east side. In 1893, she initiated a home nursing service to help poor immigrant families living in deplorable conditions. This was the first public nursing system in the world.

In 1879, Mary Mahoney became the first black nurse when she graduated from a training program in New England. As a student, she had endured sixteen hours of backbreaking labor every day, seven days a week. The program was so difficult that only three out of a class of forty graduated.

It was inspiring to learn about the pioneers in nursing and how nursing was evolving as a profession. Other factors were also taking place that would help define nursing.

In 1894, nursing school administrators formed the American Society of Superintendents of Training Schools for Nurses to establish and maintain a universal standard for training. Three years later, nurses formed the Associated Alumnae of Trained Nurses of the United States and Canada, later called The American Nurses Association (ANA). Their goal was to elevate the standards of nursing education and establish a code of ethics. They published their first journal, the *American Journal of Nursing,* in 1900 to keep nurses informed of changes in nursing practice. In 1912, the American Society of Superintendents of Training Schools for Nurses changed its name to the National League of Nursing Education.

It wasn't until 1952 that the first issue of *Nursing Research* was published by the University of North Carolina. In 1953, the American Journal of Nursing Company published the first copy of *Nursing Outlook*— the official journal of the National League for Nursing, with a focus on nursing education—less than ten years before I entered nursing school. I felt I was in on the leading edge of changes taking place and chose to join the National Student Nurses Association and subscribed to the *American Journal of Nursing.*

In early March, Mrs. Davis announced Judy Boone and I had been selected to attend the National Student Nurses Association 1964 Convention in Atlantic City, New Jersey, on June 12 through June 15. Miss Slusser would be accompanying us as our chaperone. Since we would be close to New York, we asked if we could take a few extra days to go to the world's fair. Permission was granted. I had never flown, been to New Jersey or New York City, or seen the Atlantic Ocean. I was thrilled to be honored with this opportunity. The school paid for the trip to Atlantic City. Judy and I had to get enough money to pay for our trip from Atlantic City to New York and to cover the expenses we incurred in New York.

I was broke and eager to earn some money. Babysitting jobs were posted on the dormitory bulletin board, but I couldn't envision earning enough money babysitting. Dad peddled apples door to door when he needed extra cash. As a child, I had watched him come home with a pocketful of money. Thinking that could be the answer to my cash problems, I asked him if I could sell apples. He agreed to help me. Within two months, working Saturdays only, I had earned enough money for my trip.

Riveted with excitement and fear, Judy and I boarded our plane in Cleveland. The doors closed, a fasten seat belts sign lit up, and the plane began to move. A stewardess announced, "Good morning, ladies and gentlemen, and welcome aboard. Everybody must be seated with your seat belts fastened and tray tables in the upright position before takeoff."

She continued to give instructions on what to do in the event of an emergency as she demonstrated the use of an oxygen mask and a flotation cushion. My anxiety increased as I imagined what could go wrong. The plane halted at the end of the runway and then, suddenly, the engines roared and the plane moved, quickly accelerating and lifting off the ground. I gawked through the window until I could see only the fluffy, white clouds below.

Atlantic City was breathtaking. People bustled in and out of shops. Others strolled along the boardwalk. Lights flashed. Smells of food and ocean water filled the air. The beach beckoned us. Walking from our hotel across the boardwalk and down a few steps, we were on the sand. Shedding our shoes, we dipped our toes in the freezing water and shrilled with excitement. It was all about earning bragging rights.

Business meetings, discussions, and planning sessions filled our days. Nursing shortages were widespread and nursing schools restricted admission of certain groups. Married persons and males were excluded. I knew that but had totally lacked a conscious awareness of the exclusion of blacks. At MB Johnson, we were an all-white group of single, young females. The National League for Nursing reported the number of black students enrolled in nursing programs was around 3 percent. The National

Student Nurses' Association recruitment committee initiated plans to get student nurses involved in recruitment practices and admission policies.

Discriminatory practices in hospitals were prevalent. Black professionals were denied staff privileges, and black students were denied access to nurse and residency training programs. Separate hospitals served the black community. Provisions for the same quality of care was lacking because money was not allocated to these hospitals to purchase state-of-the art equipment. Even hospitals with separate wards for minority groups were poorly equipped and staffed.

In 1946, the Hill–Burton Act, designed to provide federal grants and guaranteed loans to improve hospitals, had been passed. Facilities receiving funds were forbidden to discriminate based on race, color, national origin, or creed and were to provide a certain percentage of free and reduced-cost care.

In 1963, a landmark case, Simkins v. Moses H. Cone Memorial Hospital, had challenged the use of public funds to expand segregated hospitals. Moses H. Cone Hospital claimed exemption from these requirements, citing it was a private hospital. Initially, the court upheld the hospital's claims, but in a court of appeals, the ruling was overturned. It was found that Moses H. Cone was not a private hospital because the facility was receiving federal money.

In the evenings, we relished the fresh smell of ocean water and the sound of waves crashing on the shore. Judy and I planned to arise early and enjoy a bike ride on the boardwalk before our morning sessions. Miss Slusser expressed a desire to accompany us. Deciding on a designated time and place to meet in the morning, Judy and I retired for the night. In the morning, Miss Slusser didn't show up. Finding her room, we tapped lightly on the door. Getting no response, we scurried off to rent a bicycle built for two and had a fabulous time touring the boardwalk and keeping a respectable distance from our hotel. Upon returning, we found Miss Slusser standing in front of the hotel and assured her we'd tried to find her before we'd left.

After three nights in Atlantic City, Judy and I boarded a train to New York City and arrived at Grand Central Station, only two to three miles from our hotel in Manhattan and a thirty-minute taxi ride to the fairgrounds. Venturing outside our hotel, surrounded by tall buildings and losing all sense of direction, we hailed a taxi. Towering at the world's fair entrance was a huge steel ball shaped like the earth, symbolizing the theme "Peace through Understanding."

Paying the two-dollar admission fee, we entered a festival of sights, sounds, smells, and foods. Toddlers were pushed around in bright red or blue 1963 Corvette strollers. Hopping on board a small boat in the Pepsi pavilion, we journeyed through many lands to the tune of "It's a Small World," admiring animated dolls adorned in their native clothes. We rode a giant US Royal Tires Ferris wheel in a barrel-shaped gondola and ate heavenly Bel-Gen (Belgian) waffles served with whipped cream and strawberries.

Exhausted and exhilarated, we returned to our hotel for the night.

Before leaving New York, we visited the Empire State Building, Times Square, and Radio City Music Hall. There we saw the Rockettes, Rodney Dangerfield, and a movie. The whole experience was awesome. Back home, we settled into what now seemed humdrum.

I began entertaining the idea of going back to school to get my bachelor of science in nursing (BSN). After completing the professional nursing course, my mind was made up. I set my sights on becoming a professional nurse.

GRADUATION

One hundred days before graduation, we hung streamers from the ceiling in the dormitory hall, and each evening we gathered to pull down a streamer and sing, "One hundred streamers hung in the hall, one hundred streamers in all. Pull one down and pass it around; ninety-nine streamers hung in the hall."

Miss Durkin, our housemother, came and watched as we gathered and sang, "One streamer hung in the hall, one streamer in all. Pull one down and pass it around; no more streamers hung in the hall."

We screamed, cheered, and ran around celebrating our last night. Miss Durkin stood by, clapping her hands and smiling. Remembering the first day we met, I thought, *She's not the mean person I judged her to be.*

Graduation day—after meticulously folding my freshly starched nursing cap and admiring my new all-white uniform, I began getting dressed. Wearing only my undergarments, I went to the bathroom to apply some makeup.

Judy was in the bathroom and said, "You have your slip on inside out."

Chuckling, I asked, "Do you think I'm ready to be a nurse?" and started pulling it off.

"Stop. That means good luck."

"What?"

"Wearing it inside out. If you change it, you'll have bad luck."

"I'm not superstitious," I said but left it as it was.

The First Congregational Church sanctuary was packed with family and friends when we walked in and took our seats in the chancel area. Speeches were delivered and special awards were presented. My name was called as the recipient of the Outstanding Graduate Award, selected by the hospital staff and doctors. Totally taken by surprise, I stepped forward to receive a gold Nightingale Lamp pin. Mrs. Davis congratulated me and pinned it on my uniform. Returning to my seat, I remembered my slip was inside out.

While I was talking with my family and friends during the reception following the ceremony, a man walked up to me and asked, "Do you know who I am?"

"Don't tell me. Give me a second to think." He looked familiar. Oh yeah, I had taken care of him my freshman year after he had suffered a heart attack. "Mr. Dempsey, I'm so glad to see you," I said and gave him a hug.

"I wanted to come and celebrate with you."

"Thanks. This means a lot to me. How are you doing?"

"I'm doing well. I'm back to work and walking a mile every day. My doctor says I'm a lucky man. I think I am too."

"You look great."

"I've lost twenty-five pounds and quit smoking."

"Good for you."

He smiled, gave me a hug, and wished me well before leaving.

Following the reception, I returned to the dorm and finished packing, said my goodbyes, cried, and laughed. By the time I got home, I was exhausted. My emotions had been swinging from highs to lows since the day had started, and had all worn me to a frazzle. Plopping down in a chair, I reminisced until I nodded off.

In a week, I would be starting my night shift job on pediatrics at Elyria

Memorial Hospital as a graduate nurse. I practiced signing my name, Miss Swan, GN, and dreamed of the day I could legally write RN after my name, which was at least two months in the future. My state board examination was scheduled a month from now, and it would be at least another month waiting for the results.

Before starting my job, I spent all my money purchasing white uniforms (only dresses were available) and a new pair of Clinic Shoes. Being completely broke, I spent the rest of my time reading some good books, basking in the sun, and gardening. I was rested, relaxed, anxious, and excited when I reported for duty.

Mrs. Allen, RN, probably in her late twenties to early thirties, greeted me at the pediatric unit at Elyria Memorial Hospital, in Elyria, Ohio, with "Welcome. I'm glad to see you." We were the only nurses on the unit.

"I'm thrilled to be here."

"Fantastic. Let's listen to the evening shift report, and then I'll go over the night routine with you."

She divided the patients equally and gave me the least complicated ones. I had nine patients. Two of them were in croup tents. Throughout the night, she touched base with me and answered my questions. I was grateful for her help and decided I would enjoy working with her. My first night went smoothly and without too much stress. There were no emergencies, and the children slept well. The last two hours of the night shift were the busiest, trying to get everything done—changing sheets and gowns on my two patients in croup tents, filling the tents with fresh ice, changing out the oxygen tanks, administering 6:00 a.m. medications, bathing and preparing a two-year-old for surgery, finishing my charting, and giving report. I was ready to leave and get some sleep.

My body was exhausted, but my mind wouldn't shut down. After tossing and turning for several hours, I finally drifted off and woke up two hours later. I lay in bed for another hour before giving up and getting up. Before going to work, I was able to seize two additional hours of sleep.

Most nights were routine. Tonight was not. The supervisor was on the unit and greeted me with "I'm sending you to 4 North to stay with a patient. He was in a motorcycle accident and will be brought to his room from the recovery room in a few minutes."

My heart skipped two beats. She continued to tell me about him while walking with me to the unit.

"He's eighteen years old and has multiple cuts and broken bones. The most severe injury is a lacerated jugular vein. Alberta Davis, the nursing school director, witnessed the accident, jumped out of her car, rushed to the scene, and immediately applied pressure on his neck until help arrived. She saved his life. He has a tracheotomy and is receiving blood transfusions."

I was on edge and started sweating.

She had briefed me well. The patient looked just like I'd anticipated. Along with a large bulging dressing on his neck and a fresh tracheotomy, he had multiple abrasions on his face and entire body and splints on both arms and his left leg, as well as IV tubes and a urinary catheter. He was conscious.

As soon as the recovery room nurse finished reporting on his condition, I dove into action, checking dressings and vital signs, suctioning the tracheotomy, measuring intake and output every hour, changing IV solutions, and administering pain medication. The night flew by.

Around six in the morning, Mrs. Davis stopped by to check on his condition and to talk to him.

She stood by his bed and said, "I'm Alberta Davis. I saw the accident. The lady told the police it was your fault. I set the record straight. It wasn't your fault. Here's my phone number if you need me as a witness."

She laid a piece of paper with her name and phone number on his bedside table.

"Mr. Arnold, Mrs. Davis is a nurse. She gave you first aid until the ambulance got there," I said.

He mouthed, "Thank you," to Mrs. Davis.

"I'd give you a big hug, but there's no place for me to get my arms around you," she said.

He attempted to smile.

Mrs. Davis left, and I completed his care. The next night, I was back on the pediatric unit and never had the privilege of caring for Mr. Arnold again. I stopped by his room a couple of times before leaving in the mornings. He was making a slow recovery and, on one occasion, told me how grateful he was for Mrs. Davis.

Judy Boone and I rode together to Columbus, Ohio, in a car she had purchased after graduation. Ready or not, we were on our way to take our state board licensing exam. We arrived the evening before the exam and found our classmates. Very little time was spent catching up; instead, we talked about the exam and possible questions. My anxiety increased as topics were brought up that I had forgotten all about. I wished I had taken time to study. We retired early for a good night's sleep.

Testing on five separate subjects (medical, surgical, obstetric, pediatric, and psychiatric nursing) would begin in the morning and last one and a half days. We were scheduled to take two exams before lunch, two after lunch, and two the next morning. The last exam on the second day was not part of our licensing exam. It was given to test the reliability and validity of proposed new questions for future use on the licensing examinations.

Judy and I were up bright and early. After breakfast, we headed to the exam site and joined hundreds of others in line for admission to the exam room. One and a half hours were allotted for each exam. We could leave the room as soon as we finished. Some were leaving the room after an hour. Was I slow or not as smart as them? It took me an hour and a half to complete the first exam.

I found some of my classmates and asked, "What did you think of the test?"

They began asking how I answered specific questions. We agreed on many of our answers but not all of them. I felt less confident the longer we debated.

That didn't stop us from repeating the same routine after every exam. After completing our last test, we said our goodbyes and went our separate ways.

Five weeks later, I received an envelope from the Ohio State Board of Nursing. Rushing into the house with excitement I yelled, "I got my state board results!" and sat down before opening the envelope. The first paper I spied was my temporary license to practice as a registered nurse. Everyone in town probably heard me jubilate, "I passed!"

My mother was standing in front of me. I hadn't seen her come into the room.

"Congratulations. I knew you would."

"You did? I didn't."

She just stood there, smiling.

Rummaging through all the papers, I found my scores. I had scored over five hundred on each test, meaning I'd made nationals. I could practice nursing in every state by applying for that state's license. No need to repeat the examination.

Today, graduates take their exam, called the National Council Licensure Examination (NCLEX-RN) on a computer at a testing site. There are 265 questions. After answering 75 questions, the computer determines the level of competency. If competent, the exam is over. If not, questions continue to pop up until competency is established or until all the questions are answered or time expires. It still takes a month to get the official results because answers are scored a second time at the testing center.

My fiancé, Byron, was stationed at Camp Lejeune, North Carolina. Our courtship was long distance. Whenever possible, he made it home for a weekend. We talked about getting married after I graduated and decided to begin making plans.

In September, he received orders to go to Vietnam. He would be leaving in October. We put our plans on hold.

He was able to come home for a couple of weeks before departing. We spent a few wonderful weeks together, the longest we had been together in three years. I went with him and his father to the airport. When he walked off to board the plane, I burst into tears. His dad put his arm around me, trying to console me. I couldn't stop crying. The entire ride back home, all I could see was him walking away and I couldn't keep from wondering if I would ever see him alive again.

I had been entertaining the idea of getting my bachelor of science in nursing and decided to move forward with that plan since Byron would be gone for thirteen months. I decided to apply for admission at Ohio State University. My sister Joyce, recently divorced, was living in Worthington, Ohio, only a few miles from the campus. I contacted her, and we talked about my plans. Joyce offered me a job watching her children in the evenings while she was at work, in exchange for room and board. I accepted her offer.

A few weeks after sending my application to Ohio State, I received a letter acknowledging receipt of my application. However, OSU was missing my MB Johnson School of Nursing transcripts. I contacted the school and was informed my transcripts had been sent but the school would resend them.

Three to four weeks later, I received another request for transcripts. My nursing school honored my request once again and sent the transcripts.

Time passed with no word from Ohio State. My plans were to begin pursuing my BSN in the winter quarter. I resigned from my job at Elyria Memorial Hospital and moved to Columbus at the end of December 1964. No one, including Joyce or Mom, knew that I had not been officially accepted at Ohio State.

THE OHIO STATE UNIVERSITY

With all my belongings packed and ready to move, my parents drove me to the large older house Joyce was renting. It was a half block from High Street, the main street running to the Ohio State University campus and to downtown Columbus. Buses ran every seven minutes. It was perfect. I was tingling with excitement.

Joyce, an industrial nurse, worked the evening shift at the Ohio Malleable Iron Company. Recently divorced with three young children, ages five, three, and one years old, she was excited for me and began asking questions.

"What classes are you taking this quarter?"

"I don't know."

"Aren't you signed up?"

"No. I'll be going to the university tomorrow morning to get everything lined up."

"I thought you were supposed to be signed up by now."

"Really? No one told me."

"That's strange."

Early the following morning, with a map of the Ohio State campus in my hand, I boarded a bus. The campus was huge. I began wondering what I had gotten myself into. Walking into the admissions office, I said to a woman behind a desk, "Hi, my name is Nancy Swan. I'm here to start classes this quarter, but I haven't received an acceptance letter."

She looked at me strangely and said, "You're here to start classes but haven't been accepted?"

Suddenly I felt pretty stupid.

"That's correct. I sent my application and received two letters requesting my transcripts from the MB Johnson School of Nursing. The nursing school secretary assured me they were sent on three different occasions. I didn't know what else to do, so I quit my job and moved to Columbus to get this straightened out and start school."

Emphasizing the seriousness of the situation, she adjusted her glasses with both hands while scrutinizing me intently. "What's your full name and date of birth?"

"Nancy Lou Swan. September 22, 1943." As she was writing down the information, I made a mental note of the name, Mrs. Burgess, printed on her name tag.

Motioning to some chairs, she said, "Have a seat. I'll check into it."

"Thanks," I said and strutted over to a chair.

Thirty to forty-five minutes later, Mrs. Burgess called my name. I bounced out of my chair and scurried over to her.

"We found your application and transcripts and have looked through them. You are officially accepted. Congratulations."

Restraining from screaming with joy, I said, "Thank you, thank you so much. You're a godsend."

"You're welcome," she said, smiling. "The next thing you need to do is meet with an adviser. I don't know how long this will take." Mrs. Burgess handed me the school catalog and said, "Go ahead and start looking through this while you wait."

Sitting down once again, I began searching through the catalog. It took a few minutes for me to figure out the School of Nursing was under the College of Medicine. I began looking at all the prerequisites needed before enrolling in nursing courses. Lucky me. I had already taken many of the courses.

Thirty minutes passed before Mrs. Burgess reappeared. "I've set you up to see Mrs. Jacobs. If you hurry over to her office, she can see you this morning." She marked a red X on the campus map and said, "This is where you are." She placed another red X on the map and said, "This is where you can find Mrs. Jacobs." Placing the map and my files in my hand she said, "Good luck."

"Thanks." That sounded trite. No amount of thanks could express the magnitude of my gratitude.

Twenty minutes later, I was seated in a reception room waiting to see Mrs. Jacobs. A middle-aged female popped her head out of an office door and said, "Miss Swan." I stood up, and she motioned for me to come to her office. She took the file from my hand, smiled, and said, "Congratulations. I understand you were accepted for admission this morning. My name is Mrs. Jacobs. It will take me a few minutes to look through your file."

She began shuffling through the papers and jotting down some notes. I made a conscious effort to look calm—quite opposite from what I was feeling. What was she writing?

Finally, she looked at me and said, "Before I can sign you up for courses, you need to take some placement tests. Have a seat in the lobby while I get you scheduled."

Placement tests? I didn't know what she was talking about.

A few minutes later, Mrs. Jacobs found me. "You're scheduled to take the English placement test at 1:00 p.m. today and the math placement test at 8:00 a.m. tomorrow. Get to the testing site about ten minutes early. Come back to my office after you have taken the tests, and we'll get you signed up for your courses."

The following afternoon, Mrs. Jacobs apprised me of my test results. "You passed the English test, but you will need to take a remedial math course."

Being both surprised and disappointed because math had been one of my strengths in high school, I was even more disappointed to learn that none of my Oberlin College courses would transfer because they were taught contractually to MB Johnson students and not offered to Oberlin College enrollees. Thankfully, all my nursing courses transferred. It would take two full years to earn my bachelor of science in nursing.

Searching through the catalog, we selected my courses for the winter quarter. I would have to wait until the spring quarter to take the remedial math course because all the classes were full. Two quarters of physical education were required. Physical fitness was the only course left with any spaces, so I signed up for that class. Once my schedule was complete, I was sent to the registrar's office to pay my tuition and to the bookstore to purchase my books.

Tuition was $125 plus a few extra bucks for lab fees. At the bookstore, I spent an additional $35 on books and then boarded a bus back to my sister's house.

In addition to babysitting, I needed an income to pay for my personal expenses and college fees. I applied at Memorial Hospital and was hired for an RN weekend evening position.

Just in the nick of time, all arrangements were in place. My classes commenced in the morning. Eager to get started, I was up early the next morning checking my schedule and the location of my classes. English composition was my first class. My clearest memory of this class is Professor Walters saying, "James Thurber flunked this course."

My stress level increased. I thought that, if James Thurber couldn't pass this course, I didn't stand a chance.

After English class, I was ready to have some fun in my fitness class. What was I thinking? I should have known there was a reason for the open spaces. The first order of business was to have a picture taken of my naked body with full frontal, back, and side views. We were assured the photos and negatives would be destroyed at the end of the quarter. The photos would be available for me to see at my next class, and I was to develop a personal fitness plan based on what I saw. I would have dropped the course if I hadn't needed to get the physical education requirement completed in my first two quarters.

After lunch, I attended my psychology class before returning home to watch the kids. I had been hashing over in my mind how I would take care of the kids and get my homework done. My goal was to have them in bed by eight o'clock, allowing time for me to study.

I picked up Marie and Paul from the neighbor and played with them while waiting for David to get home from school. Joyce made it easy for me to prepare meals and snacks by having a list of what to serve each evening. After dinner, I tidied up the kitchen and helped David with his homework, while Marie and Paul entertained themselves.

Paul was bathed and in bed at seven thirty. By eight o'clock, all the kids were in bed, and I sat down to study. Joyce arrived home around midnight and found me studying at the kitchen table. We talked briefly before I excused myself to get ready for bed. I stuck with this routine the entire time I stayed with Joyce with the exception of watching two television shows a week—*Password* and *The Andy Williams Show*.

Saturday rolled around quickly. In the morning, I wrote a long letter to Byron detailing my move to Columbus, starting classes, and getting ready to begin a new job at Memorial Hospital. I longed for his return and hoped time would pass quickly. He was due back in the states in late November. It was only January.

I took a bus and walked the remainder of the way, about two and a half blocks, to the hospital. I had planned to take a bus to and from work, but once I was at the hospital I was informed, "Do not leave the hospital alone at night. Last year, one of our nurses was raped in the parking lot."

That scared me. I splurged and took a taxi home.

Working at the hospital was a nice break from school and babysitting. I was doing what I loved.

One evening, the nursing supervisor pulled me to a different unit, where there had been four admissions just prior to the shift change and a nurse had called out sick. After report, I made rounds to meet my assigned patients.

"Hi, Mrs. Hubbell. My name is Miss Swan. I'll be your nurse this evening."

"That isn't my name. I'm Mrs. Rogers."

"Did you notice your wristband has you identified as Mrs. Hubbell?"

"No. Do you know why I'm here?"

"Let me look at my assignment and see what I was told about you, Mrs. Rogers. Oh yes, I see you are here for a blood clot in your left leg."

"That's correct," she said looking a little relieved.

"I'm going to go and get this straightened out."

I left her room and told the head nurse, who called the nursing supervisor. While I was waiting for the nursing supervisor to arrive I went to the room my assignment sheet indicated was Mrs. Rogers's room.

"Hello," I said while lifting her hand to check the wristband and saw Mrs. Rogers's name. "Tell me your name,"

"Mrs. Hubbell."

"Mrs. Hubbell, my name is Miss Swan. I'm your nurse this evening. Your wristband has the wrong name. I'll get it corrected. I understand you're here for the treatment of congestive heart failure."

"That's right."

"Do you need anything?"

"No. I just want to get some rest."

"Okay. I'll be back as soon as I have a new wristband for you."

The nursing supervisor was in the nursing station waiting for me and said, "I got called because one of your new admissions has the wrong wristband. You need to be more careful. Do you know how serious this is?"

"Yes, but I didn't put those wristbands on."

"Who put them on?"

"I don't know. They were like this when I went around to meet my patients after report."

"Who gave you report?"

"I don't know."

"You don't know who gave you report?" she said in a way that was intended for me to feel stupid.

"No. This is my first time on this unit, and I don't recall the nurse's name," I said. *She ought to be thanking me for finding the mistake*, I thought, and restrained myself from telling her that.

Pivoting around, she walked away in a huff.

I stood in the station, not sure what to do next. Was she getting new wristbands or was I supposed to call the admission office? Deciding to wait and see, I went to meet the rest of my patients.

Today, patient wristbands are applied in the admission office.

Mr. Russo was in the hospital for treatment of thalassemia, an inherited blood disorder that causes anemia. There are two classifications of thalassemia—major and minor. The life expectancy for thalassemia major is only a few years. Thalassemia minor has varying degrees of severity, ranging from no symptoms to needing frequent blood transfusions. Mr. Russo was in the hospital for a blood transfusion for the minor form. In an effort to reduce allergic reactions, his doctor had ordered packed red blood cells, rather than whole blood. I noticed he was receiving whole blood and immediately clamped the whole blood IV tubing and opened the normal saline solution tubing to keep the vein open.

Mr. Russo asked, "What are you doing?"

"I switched your IV over to normal saline. This looks like whole blood."

"I'm not supposed to get whole blood."

"I know. That's why I stopped it. Do you feel okay?"

"Yes."

"Good. I'm going to go check this out. Here's your call bell. Let me know if you start to feel differently. I'll be back in a few minutes."

Once again, I reported my finding and actions to the head nurse.

"Go check his vital signs and stay with him. I'll call his doctor and the nursing supervisor."

Mr. Russo's vital signs were normal. I stayed with him until I was summoned to the nursing station.

The patient's doctor was standing in the station. He began pounding on the wall and yelling, "Why are you trying to kill my patient?"

Everyone nearby, including visitors, stopped to gawk.

Being the new kid on their block, I was getting blamed for the mistakes. I wanted to scream. Instead, I said, "I'm not trying to kill your patient. The whole blood was running when I arrived for duty this evening."

Dr. Ingle calmed down and took me with him to check on Mr. Russo. Since Mr. Russo had only received a small amount of the whole blood, Dr. Ingle ordered another unit of packed blood cells. I hung them after double-checking, first with the laboratory staff and then with the head nurse, to ensure the right product was given to me.

The remainder of the shift went smoothly, although I had to play catch-up. I was physically and mentally exhausted by the time I finished.

Classes were going well. Taking psychology and sociology courses again was not as boring as I had surmised it might be. A few years under my belt had given me a new perspective on understanding and applying the concepts in my work. My music appreciation class was pure enjoyment, and the English course was a lot easier than the instructor had made it out to be on that first day. Unlike James Thurber, I passed the course with a B.

Five months after I began working at Memorial Hospital, I was transferred to an eye, ears, nose, and throat (EENT) unit. On the weekend evening shifts, I was the only registered nurse on the unit.

Dr. Knight was a plastic surgeon. Most of his patients were hospitalized for rhinoplastics (nose jobs). Nearly every time Dr. Knight made rounds, he would look at me intently as if examining my nose and say, "I could give you a pretty nose."

It was creepy. But trying to be cordial, I always responded with "No thanks."

Mrs. O'Keeffe was recovering from cataract surgery. My experience was limited to book knowledge and classroom teaching. She was on complete bed rest and was to lie flat on her back except at mealtime, when the head of the bed could be raised thirty degrees. Sandbags were placed on each side of her head to prevent her from turning her head from side to side.

Her surgeon stopped by to make rounds. Mrs. O'Keeffe's roommate was watching TV when the doctor and I entered the room. He looked at me and asked angrily, "Why is the TV on?"

His tone of voice cued me in that there was a problem. Being at a loss for words, I remained silent. He marched over to the TV, turned it off, swiveled around looking directly at me, and said in a stern voice, "She's to keep her eyes at rest. Eye movement can cause bleeding." After examining her eye, he declared, "It looks good. No signs of bleeding."

Feeling relieved, I mustered up the courage to ask if it would be okay to pull the curtain around Mrs. O'Keeffe bed and let her roommate watch TV.

"That would be okay. Be sure to keep the curtain pulled."

"I will."

After he left, Mrs. O'Keeffe's roommate said, "Thanks."

I applied for a stipend. If I got it, all my tuition and books would be paid in full for my last four quarters, and I would receive $200 a month for living expenses. There were two stipulations: I was not allowed to work during that time, and I would agree to practice nursing for at least three years after graduation.

Sitting at my desk studying, I heard a knock on my door. It was unusual for any of my friends to drop by during the week. I looked through the peephole, saw Byron standing there, and nearly fainted. We embraced one another without saying a word. Finally, I asked him to come in.

"Why didn't you tell me you were home?"

"I wanted to surprise you."

"You did and almost gave me a heart attack! When did you get back?"

"Yesterday. I flew into Cleveland and surprised Mom and Dad, too."

We went out to a nice restaurant, talked incessantly, and ate a little. He had orders to go to the El Toro Air Station in Southern California and would be leaving in a couple of weeks. I made plans to go home for Thanksgiving weekend and spend time with him before he left once again.

I got through the next week. Once again, we had a wonderful time and then it was time to return to Columbus. Byron had left for California. I wondered how much more of this I could endure.

On returning to Columbus, I received great news! I had gotten the stipend. Immediately, I began making plans to move to an apartment near campus and resign from my job at Memorial Hospital, allowing flexibility in scheduling classes, more time to study, and even the ability to attend some Ohio State basketball games. I was euphoric.

One of my classmates, Sylvia, was looking for an apartment too. We decided to share an apartment and found one fully furnished for ninety-five dollars a month. It was directly across the street from the university. I resigned from my job at Memorial Hospital effective the third week in December 1965 and had time to go home for a relaxing Christmas holiday.

Returning to Columbus recharged, I settled into the apartment before classes started. I was already missing my sister, the kids, and my job.

In nutrition class, we were required to read five journal articles a week and summarize the contents on index cards for our instructor's review. My apartment was a blessing. I could easily get to the library at any time. I suspected the instructor did not have time to read all the cards turned in each week, so, as a way to test my assumption, I wrote lines from nursery rhymes in the middle of some of the cards. My cards were returned with check marks and no comments about the content.

Anatomy classes were a breeze compared to the physiology classes. I had my own formaldehyde-preserved cat to dissect. It didn't look like a cat by the time the course ended, and the smell of the formaldehyde was sickening.

We had a human cadaver in the lab, which had been already dissected by a med student but was available for viewing human anatomical parts. The first time the instructor reeled it up from its formaldehyde bed, I felt queasy. The body and all the exposed parts had the color of a dead, featherless chicken. I tried not to think of it as once having been a live human being. That made it more bearable, but I never felt completely at ease viewing the cadaver.

The two quarters of physiology classes were grueling and more comprehensive than the combined anatomy and physiology courses at Oberlin College. There were no familiar faces in the large classroom of more than one hundred students. One brilliant premed student aced all the exams. I made it a point to get to know him and ask questions, but his knowledge never osmosed to my cells. For the first time in my life, I was thankful to make a C in a course.

All around campus, students were raving about the new series, *Batman*. I did not have a TV, so on one Thursday evening, I postponed doing my homework and sauntered down to the student union and joined the standing room only crowd in front of the TV. The pack cheered when Batman and Robin sped out of their cave in the Batmobile. The words *pow*, *kaboom*, and *bam* appeared on the screen when they slugged the villains. The group went wild with whooping and hollering. Late that night, after finishing my homework, I decided it wasn't worth watching *Batman* again.

In spring 1966, I was assigned to work for two weeks in a tuberculosis hospital as part of my communicable disease course. A tine test was required before starting the course. It consisted of pricking my forearm with a button-shaped object with four to six tiny needles coated with the tuberculosis antigen. Previous exposure to the tubercle bacillus (the organism causing TB) would cause an allergic reaction at the test site within two to three days (a positive skin test). A clearly defined hardened area under my skin would denote the live bacteria had invaded my body. It could be active or it could be encapsulated in my lung (inactive). Only a follow-up chest x-ray and sputum tests could confirm an active case. Fortunately, mine was negative. What a relief.

If the test was positive and the bacteria were walled off, they were still reproducing and could break free many years later. A regimen of drugs taken for an entire year would increase the probability of keeping it encapsulated by preventing it from reproducing.

The TB hospital was a small facility, unlike the large sanatoriums of the past. There had been a decline in admissions to TB hospitals with the advent of drugs for treatment. A nurse greeted me and took me on a tour of the facility after I donned a mask and gown. Still feeling antsy and fearful of getting TB, I asked her, "How many of the staff have contracted TB while working here?"

"That's a common question, but I can honestly tell you no one. We know how to prevent the spread. Just follow our procedures and you'll be okay. The real danger occurs when you are in close contact with someone with an active case and don't know it."

I followed her around all day. Patients who could not be adequately cared for at home were admitted for treatment, rest, good nutrition, and education about the TB. Some patients needed surgery to remove a lobe of the lung or to collapse a lung, depending on the severity of the TB. The lengths of stay varied from a few months to a year or longer.

I was like a sponge, attending patient classes and soaking up information. Most of my time was spent helping patients with daily hygiene, making beds, cleaning rooms, administering medications, and collecting sputum specimens. I observed patient interactions and saw many friendships develop, knowing they would last a lifetime. On my last day, I taught a class on preventing the spread of TB. The patients came to the classroom carrying their Kleenex and paper bags and sat attentively as we talked about going home to their spouses and children. Some cried with joy at the thought of reuniting with their families. I felt a tear trickle down my cheek. My fiancé was stationed in southern California. We had begun making plans to tie the knot and set a date for December 17, three days before my graduation. My hopes and dreams were that Byron and I would never be apart again. I knew the pain of separation.

Summer quarter rolled around quickly, and I enrolled in a course called Coordinated Care. Given the option of choosing a hospital unit, I selected the neurology unit, the one unit I knew the least about. It sounded exciting, challenging, and the perfect setting for expanding my horizons. The focus in this course was to learn about the many services available for patients in the hospital and community and coordinating their care utilizing these services.

My assignment was to lead a team of nurses and aides caring for a group of patients. Making decisions on each team member's assignment was frustrating. Some team members were opposed to working with their assigned patients, claiming a patient was too demanding or did not like them.

That information provided fuel for our conferences. Why did they think the patient was demanding? Could it be the patient's fear or lack of control over his or her life? What could we do to allay our patients' fears or give them more control?

We were caring for patients with head injuries, strokes, brain tumors, and spinal cord injuries. I allowed the staff members to express their frustrations and encouraged them to put themselves in their patients' place. What would they need? Who had the qualities to work best with a demanding patient? What could they learn from the experience?

I shared with them my feelings of frustration and fear, my lack of confidence in caring for some of the patients, and my admiration of their expertise. The care they were providing was extremely challenging and often depressing. They began sharing their successes and teaching me.

As a team, we were able to suggest services for hospitalized patients. Some needed speech therapy, others occupational and physical therapy. Still others, after discharge, would need visiting nurses or vocational rehabilitation. Our team shared identified needs with the physicians, who were often willing to make the referrals.

Many days, I left the hospital exhausted from all the physical and mental exertion. I needed to take care of myself and spent time getting together with my friends just to laugh and have a good time.

Overall, this course and my choice of the neurology unit provided an invaluable experience that has helped me throughout my nursing career.

Between the summer and fall quarter, I went home to finalize my wedding plans. Only one quarter to go before graduating and getting married. After a hectic few days at home, I returned to Columbus and began my last nursing course, Public Health Nursing.

After reviewing in the classroom everything in my bag and how to do a well baby checkup, I was raring to go. For the first time, I ventured outside a hospital setting and was on my own visiting patients in their homes. Wearing my white uniform with a badge identifying me as a public health nurse and carrying a black bag with supplies, I boarded a bus to a lower-income section of the city to see my first patient—Sharon, a seventeen-year-old with a newborn baby girl.

A pretty young girl answered the door.

"Hi. My name is Miss Swan. Is Sharon home?"

"That's me. Come on in. A nurse at the hospital said someone would be stopping by to check my baby."

"Good. I'm glad I didn't catch you by surprise."

She led me to a sofa where we sat down and chatted.

"How are you getting along?"

"Fine. I'm just tired. My mom helps out, but I get up in the night to feed Dana. She only sleeps about two to three hours at a time."

"That's not much. I guess that's all the sleep you get too?"

"Yeah."

"Well, I'll try to get done as quickly as possible so you can get some rest. Where is Dana?"

"She's asleep."

"Do you have a table where I can lay out a small sheet and check Dana?"

She took me to the kitchen and cleared and wiped the table.

"That's perfect," I said as I laid my tape measure on a corner of the sheet. "Can you get her for me to examine?"

I used the wipes from my bag to clean my hands while she was gone.

Sharon returned carrying her sleeping baby. She was holding her just right, supporting her back, head, and neck.

"She's beautiful."

"Thanks."

"Lay her here on the table."

She gently placed her on the sheet. Dana woke up and began to cry.

"I'm sorry. Do you think she'll go back to sleep when I leave?"

"I hope so."

After checking her temperature, breathing, and pulse, I palpated Dana's anterior fontanel and said, "This is her soft spot. It should be closed by the time she is eighteen months old. It feels and looks good."

"I can see her heart beating in it. Is that normal?"

"Yes. The main thing is it shouldn't be caved in or bulging. Sunken or caved in means she's dehydrated and needs more fluids. Bulging when she isn't crying could indicate increased pressure in her skull. If that happens, call your pediatrician."

I looked Dana over from head to toe. "Everything looks good. You can pick her up. Do you have any questions?"

She tenderly lifted the baby in her arms. "When can I give her a tub bath?"

"After the umbilical cord falls off. It will fall off on its own. Don't try to pull it off, even if it's hanging loosely. After it falls off, there may be some little pieces left behind. They will fall off on their own too. Right now, the main thing is to keep the area dry. I noticed you had her diaper folded down to keep it from rubbing or getting it wet."

"My mom taught me to do that. When will it fall off?"

"By the time she's a month old. Probably sooner. It looks nice and dry. It might fall off next week. Do you have any more questions?"

"No."

"How about you? Are you having any problems?"

"No."

"Okay. It looks like you're doing a great job taking care of her. At the hospital, did they tell you about taking her to a well baby clinic for checkups and immunizations?"

"They gave me a paper with information. I'm supposed to take her when she is six weeks old."

"It's a wonderful service. Write down all your questions before you go so you don't forget anything."

I left feeling good about the visit.

In addition to making home visits, I worked in a well baby clinic once a week. The clinic had a program for expectant parents. I was asked to teach a four-week course, which met for two hours a week in the evenings. We talked about what to expect in labor and delivery, what expecting parents needed in preparation for their baby's arrival home, breastfeeding versus formula-fed babies, and introducing new foods to the baby's diet. The parents practiced bathing and diapering a baby doll.

One evening, an expectant father asked, "Can two brown-eyed parents have a blue-eyed baby?"

He and his wife had brown eyes. Was he questioning his wife's fidelity?

In my nervousness, I couldn't reason through the answer. Finally I said, "I'm not sure. I'll check it out and answer your question in our next class."

On my way home, the answer came to me. Of course they could have a blue-eyed baby if both of them had a recessive blue-eyed gene and each passed on the recessive gene to their baby. I was relieved to be able to tell them yes in our next class.

Jackson, only six years old, had diabetes mellitus. My job was to help his mom teach him how to give himself insulin injections.

We sat down at the kitchen table. "Jackson, have you ever held a needle and syringe?"

"No."

"Okay. That's where we'll start." His mom got a syringe and needle. "This week, I want you to practice putting the needle on the syringe without touching the shiny part of the needle and learn how to read the marks on the syringe," I said while demonstrating putting the needle on the syringe. "When I come back next week, you can show me what you've learned. For example, I might ask you to show me the mark on the syringe for ten units. Your mom can help you learn all the marks."

"Okay," he said, smiling.

"Mom, do you have any questions?"

"No. I can teach him that."

"Next week, I'll bring an orange and a vial of water for him to practice giving a shot to an orange."

Several weeks later, Jackson greeted me with "I gave my insulin shot this morning!"

"What! All by yourself?"

"Yes, ma'am."

"Mom, how did he do?"

"Really well."

Jackson was beaming.

"How did you get to be so smart?"

He shrugged his shoulders and smiled.

"Today is my last day. You'll have someone new next week. I'm going to miss our visits."

Jackson got up and gave me a hug.

"I'll never forget you. Can I tell my friends how smart you are?"

"Yes."

They stood at the door and waved goodbye as I walked away.

It was time for final exams. After exams, I would move my belongings back home to Elyria, Ohio; get married; and return for my graduation ceremony. It was hard to believe I would soon have a Mrs. in front of my name and a BSN after my name.

13

AFTER OHIO STATE

Four days before my wedding, I moved my belongings back home, and Murphy's law was activated. Joyce, who was to be in charge of the guest book, had emergency gallbladder surgery. Arrangements were made for one of the ushers to assume her duties. And then there was poor Sylvia, my college roommate and one of my bridesmaids. During my last quarter at Ohio State, she had to drop out of school to have a metal plate removed from her hip. It had popped loose. Unable to make her dress fitting, she arrived three days before the wedding only to discover her dress was two sizes smaller than what we had ordered. The dress shop owner scrambled to find the right fabrics and threw together a dress.

The wedding turned out beautifully, with the church adorned with hundreds of red poinsettias. A light snow was falling, and my bridesmaids were stunning in their red velvet and pink chiffon dresses and white fur mitts.

Following the reception, Byron and I drove to Columbus and danced into bliss for three days before my graduation ceremony. From there, we journeyed to Long Island, New York, to visit Byron's sister, Louise, whom he hadn't seen in several years. She had been battling breast cancer for three years, and her health was declining.

Louise, her husband, and their two teen-aged children were delighted to see us. Louise was confined to a hospital bed that had been set up in their downstairs living room. With Byron sitting by her bed, they shared fond memories until she was exhausted.

The next morning, they shed tears and said their goodbyes before we left for our road trip back to my parent's home in Elyria, Ohio. Once home, we packed a U-Haul and headed toward the El Toro Air Station in Southern California. Snowstorms hampered our travel, and Byron made arrangements for a late arrival.

After we'd settled into a small, furnished apartment in Anaheim, I applied for a job at the Orange County Medical Center in nearby Santa Ana. Nursing jobs are always available, and within two weeks, I was working the evening shift on a medical-surgical unit. Byron was working the day shift. He and I worked every third weekend but not on the same weekend. Days went by when we only saw each other late at night or early in the morning.

A month after our arrival in California, Byron received a call from his sister Dorie. Louise had died. He was not able to attend her funeral.

I began getting homesick and complained, "I want to see real trees, real houses, and real grass—not palms, dichondra, and stucco."

My love of nursing kept me going. Mr. Abrams, a thin thirty-four-year-old, was admitted with San Joaquin valley fever (coccidioidomycosis). On admission, he had a fever, weakness, and reported loss of appetite. Later, I discovered all his symptoms were typical of valley fever. When he was admitted, I knew nothing about the disease. Most of my coworkers were wonderful, but one of the older nurses criticized me by saying sarcastically, "You have a BSN. I thought you were supposed to be smart. I guess you don't know anything about Amphotericin B."

"No. I've never heard of it. I saw where it was ordered."

She rolled her eyes and said, "You need to look it up. He'll be getting it every morning."

"I'll do that. I want to learn as much as I can."

Feeling humiliated, I was determined to learn all about coccidioidomycosis. The disease is endemic to the Southwestern United States and caused by a fungus found in the soil. That explained it. They didn't teach us about San Joaquin Valley Fever in Ohio. It is contracted by inhaling the dust from soil containing the fungus. Most of the time, the disease causes an acute respiratory infection that clears on its own.

Mr. Abrams had developed a severe infection. The prognosis was poor until the discovery of Amphotericin B, a powerful antifungal drug that had to be administered intravenously. Mr. Abrams would be given increasing doses of the drug until an optimal nontoxic level was reached. Phlebitis, fever, chills, diarrhea, and respiratory distress could occur. His blood needed to be monitored for blood urea nitrogen (BUN) to determine if he was having any liver or kidney damage from the drug. I wrote the information on an index card and carried it to work with me each day until I knew it by heart.

Mr. Abrams and I developed a good rapport over the four weeks I cared for him. Each evening, I checked his vital signs, breathing, and IV site, and asked him, "Have you had any chills or diarrhea?

"Why do you ask me that every night?" he inquired.

"I want to make sure you aren't having any side effects from your medicine. So far, you're doing well."

"They have to change my IV every few days. It keeps getting red and hurts where the needle is."

"The medicine causes that. It's powerful stuff, but it's getting you better. You look healthier than the first day I saw you."

"My appetite has come back, and I've gained eight pounds. I need to gain about thirty more."

"How much weight did you lose?"

"Forty pounds."

After four weeks of treatment, Mr. Abrams was discharged. I missed him but was happy for him to be able to get back home.

One of the most challenging patients I cared for was Mrs. Carmichael. She was only forty-two years old and had colon cancer. Her surgeon had removed a portion of her colon several weeks earlier. The incision had torn open and left a gaping hole in her abdomen. The doctor debrided the wound (cut away the dead tissue) every day and packed the incision with gauze. The wound kept getting larger, and Mrs. Carmichael was getting weaker. She screamed in pain every time I changed her position. It broke my heart.

One evening, she told me, "I want to live until my daughter graduates from high school in June."

It was early May. She had a little over a month until graduation, and I wasn't sure she could survive that long. Over the next few weeks, I did everything I could to try to make her comfortable. The wound emitted the smell of rotting tissue, and her doctor wrote orders to irrigate the wound twice a day with normal saline and repack it with gauze. My whole hand fit in the large gaping hole. I'll never forget her bloodcurdling screams. She was counting down the days until graduation.

The day after her daughter's graduation, Mrs. Carmichael died. I had never seen such fortitude and had mixed emotions of relief and melancholy.

In May 1967, my husband received orders to attend polygraph school in Fort Gordon, Georgia. He would be gone for six months before returning to El Toro. Just a month before he received orders, we had bought a home in Anaheim and had been living in it for about two weeks.

I stayed behind and worked at the hospital for a few more months before deciding to apply for a position as a public health nurse. As much as I loved hospital nursing, I was determined to have a Monday through Friday day job by the time Byron came back home.

I landed the job.

Dressed in my navy blue uniform and carrying my black bag with supplies, I began making home visits. My caseload of 150 patients, mostly Hispanic, was in about a mile radius. Because many of my clients' English was limited, they had to find someone to help interpret. Within a few weeks, I enrolled in an evening Spanish course and attempted to speak some

Spanish during my home visits. My patients laughed at my efforts to try to find the right words.

Most of my clients were seen for well baby visits and discharged from our service after one or two visits. There were always more to replace them.

My supervisor gave me the name and address of a pregnant female who had tested positive for syphilis and needed treatment. I knocked on the door. A young Hispanic male opened the door.

I asked, "Is Miss Sanchez home?"

He motioned for me to come in. After stepping into the dark room, he closed the door. There was a group of young Hispanic males standing around drinking beer. No female was in sight. I wanted to run out the door, but he was standing in front of it. My heart began pounding.

In my calmest voice, I asked to see Miss Sanchez. They laughed and acted like they didn't understand English.

One of the young men tried to give me a beer.

"If she's not here, I need to go. I'll come back tomorrow," I said as I made my way around the man in front of the door and scurried out.

I had no intention of returning and reported what had happened when I returned to the office. My supervisor decided to have the police try to locate the patient. From that point on, I never entered a home until I had seen my client from the doorway and felt safe.

One of my clients, Mrs. Martinez, had leprosy. Immediately, I conjured up the image of a person wrapped in rags with a grotesque-looking face and arms stretched out in front of her shouting, "Unclean, unclean" when I came near her.

"I didn't know there were people living in the United States with leprosy," I told my supervisor.

"There aren't many, but it's found in a handful of states. Unfortunately, California is one of them. Louisiana has a leper colony."

"Are there any leper colonies in California?"

"No, and once treatment is started, it doesn't spread easily. Some physicians believe it is no longer contagious after a few weeks of treatment. I want you to stop by and see Mrs. Martinez. Find out how she's doing and whether she is taking her medicine."

Mrs. Martinez saw me coming up the walkway and stepped outside to meet me. She had several lumps on her face that she tried to hide with her hands.

"Hi, I'm Mrs. White. I stopped by to see how you're doing."

"I'm doing okay."

"Do you have enough Sulfoxone?" (This was the bacteriostatic drug used to treat leprosy. It doesn't kill the bacteria but prevents them from reproducing, and eventually they die.)

"Yes."

"I can bring some more if you need it."

"I have enough to last for another month. When I finish it, my doctor told me to stop taking it. He'll let me know when to start taking it again. He said I need rest periods every six months."

"How often do you take it?"

"I take three pills every day."

"Have you noticed any improvement?"

"The lumps are shrinking."

"That's wonderful. It's doing what it should. I'll leave my card with you, and if you need to see me, call this number," I said, handing her my card.

Returning to my car, I charted my findings before driving to see my next client. Mrs. Flores was a twenty-six-year-old who was pregnant with her seventh child. She had a history of not following through with prenatal care and showing up at the hospital in labor. My job was to encourage her to see her obstetrician and to check her blood pressure.

An attractive, young pregnant woman with dark brown hair and beaming brown eyes opened the door. A toddler, probably around two years old and the spittin' image of her mom, was clinging to Mrs. Flores's legs. Children were peering at me from a distance.

"Come in," she said as she hobbled back from the door with the girl still clasping her legs.

"Thanks. You look like you have your hands full."

We sat on the sofa, and the cushion caved in. I was practically sitting on the floor.

Mrs. Flores said, "I'm sorry. The kids have worn it out jumping around."

"It reminds me of when I was a kid and brings back good memories."

The kids had gathered around their mama. I asked them their names.

Mom prompted them to speak, but they were shy. She told me each of their names.

"I stopped by to see how you are doing. Have you been feeling okay?"

"I get tired. I can't take a nap. The kids don't let me."

"How much sleep do you get?"

"Five or six hours."

"Is your husband able to help in the evening?"

She laughed and said, "He comes home and wants to eat. Then he falls asleep. I've asked him to help. He says he works hard all day and needs rest. Sometimes he plays with the kids."

I was feeling overwhelmed just listening to her and wondering how she had time to cook, shop, clean house, do laundry, and so on.

"I need to check your blood pressure," I said, reaching into my bag to fetch the stethoscope and blood pressure cuff.

She stretched out her arm. The kids were all eyes.

"Your pressure is 128/66. That's good. Have you felt your baby move?"

"Look. Can you see it? It's moving," she said as she stretched her top taut over her abdomen.

I saw a ripple and said, "Yes. When is your baby due?"

"In about two months."

"You need to see your obstetrician during these last two months to make sure everything is going okay."

"I know. I'll try to go."

"Call and make an appointment today."

"Okay."

My gut told me she wasn't going to call.

Two weeks later, I stopped by to see her. She had not scheduled an appointment. I did what I could to check her and, again, encouraged her to see her doctor.

I began stopping by weekly. She always welcomed me.

One morning was different. Mrs. Flores started sobbing when she saw me.

"What wrong?"

"My husband had a kilo of marijuana. I burned it when he was at work. He was so mad he took all my clothes and burned them."

"What are you going to do?"

"My neighbor gave me some clothes."

"Do you feel safe?"

"Yes. He would never hurt me."

A few days later, Mrs. Flores delivered a healthy baby boy. I stopped by to see her after she got home. She and the baby were doing well. Before leaving, I asked her if she planned on having more children. She said her husband didn't believe in birth control.

Since Mrs. Flores and her baby were doing well, she was taken off my caseload. I knew I would miss her and was disappointed. We were not permitted to have a personal relationship with our clients.

Each morning, before going out, I prepared an itinerary for the day and gave it to my supervisor. When driving past Mrs. Flores home on my way to visit clients, I looked for her, hoping she would be outside where I could pull up to the curb and chat with her for a few minutes. She never was, and I never saw her again.

Byron's coworkers took me under their wings and, on weekends, invited me to their homes for dinner or a day at the beach. The wives were wonderful. They understood what it was like to be alone and made me feel like I was a part of their group.

Byron returned from Fort Gordon in late November 1967. Our job schedules afforded us time together to go to the beaches and to the mountains on weekends.

Then, in April 1968, Byron received orders to report to Camp Lejeune, North Carolina. Once again, I had mixed feelings. We had a home and friends, and I loved my job, but the thought of being closer to my family and friends in Ohio was appealing. We packed our belongings; I resigned from my job and found a real estate company to manage our property. The moving van arrived, and we set out for North Carolina.

When we reached Shreveport, Louisiana, I told my husband, "This is my kind of country. I love the trees, homes, and grass."

Arriving at Camp Lejeune in early May 1968, we were informed there was no available base housing. We found a rental home in Jacksonville and settled in.

I began working rotating shifts as a staff RN on the pediatric unit at Camp Lejeune Naval Hospital, where I saw about every type of injury, congenital anomaly, and illness. It was rare for a week to go by without caring for a child with meningitis. In the summer months, copperhead bites were prevalent.

Barry's situation caught me off guard. He was only seven months old and hospitalized with a broken femur. His tiny body was lying in bed with both legs extended at right angles to his body and connected to traction. His hips were slightly elevated off the bed, and a harness was fastened around his upper body and to the bed to keep him from becoming airborne.

While the doctor was examining Barry, he said, "Barry's broken femur was possibly caused by physical abuse. Barry's mother told the staff he rolled off the sofa. It takes a lot of force to break a femur. Mom's story just doesn't match the injury."

This was my first experience working with a child where the phrase *physical abuse* had been uttered. The doctor had to be wrong. No one could intentionally hurt a baby, could they?

While bathing and feeding Barry, I sang, "You Are My Sunshine" and called him my little cutie-pie. He looked at me and smiled. Oh how I yearned to cuddle him in my arms.

Within a few months, I cared for two more infants with a broken femur and was shocked at the prevalence of physical abuse. Why hadn't I learned about this in nursing school? We called children who were hospitalized frequently with fractures clumsy, and those who were emaciated were diagnosed with failure to thrive.

Cindy was a small, frail, two-and-a-half-year-old. The lower half of her body was badly burned. Her mother reported that she'd turned on the hot water and had accidentally scalded herself while in the bathtub. It was difficult to believe this fragile child had the strength to turn on the spigot.

I lifted her arm to apply the blood pressure cuff, and she screamed and shook uncontrollably. My speaking in a soft, calm voice did not soothe her. All efforts to comfort her were in vain.

Still, over the next several weeks, she began responding with direct eye contact and an occasional smile. Everyone was thrilled the first time she spoke, and we clapped. She clapped back.

Her discharge date was approaching. Kerry, one of the civilian nurses, felt a child abuse investigation was needed and adamantly expressed her concern to Lt. Cdr. Campbell, the nurse in charge on the unit. She assured Kerry she would speak with the hospital's commanding officer.

Any decision to initiate a formal investigation would be decided by the commander.

On the day of Cindy's discharge, the staff threw a party. We placed a party hat on Cindy, blew noisy party blowers, and ate cake and ice cream. Cindy had a blast. Her parents were invited to the party, but they arrived late and were in a hurry to take Cindy home. Cindy did not want to leave and was protesting loudly as they carried her off the unit; Nurse Kerry burst into tears.

Several weeks later, Cindy was back on the unit. Two days earlier, her mother had been admitted to the psychiatric unit, leaving her father in charge of Cindy, Cindy's one-and-a-half-year-old sister, and their six-week-old sister. In the middle of the night, he summoned an ambulance, saying he thought something was wrong with his one-and-a-half-year-old child. Upon arrival, they found the child lying listless on the floor and the other children crying. All three girls were transported to the emergency room. The middle child was pronounced dead. Cindy and her six-week-old sister were admitted to the pediatric unit. Cindy had regressed. Although not physically injured, she cowered, shook, and cried when we got near her. A physical examination of the six-week-old baby revealed vaginal tears and bleeding.

I was in shock and disbelief. The parents had been cleared to take Cindy home. Somehow, they had convinced the social worker that Cindy's burns were an accident.

A full investigation was initiated, which uncovered another death. The couple, while stationed at a different military base several years earlier, had a child who'd allegedly died from an accident.

The children's father was charged with murder and confined to the brig to await trial. This incident left an imprint on my brain and eventually would change my direction in nursing.

The Vietnam War was still raging. My husband had served one tour of duty in Vietnam while I was at Ohio State. In December 1968, he received orders to go back. My decision to stay in North Carolina wasn't easy, but the thought of uprooting again was less appealing. I had new friends in the same situation. We could support each other.

Student nurses from Onslow Technical Institute in Jacksonville rotated through the pediatric unit as part of their clinical experience, and I heard about a job opening for a nursing instructor. Teaching nursing had been a dream of mine, so I applied for the position.

A month later, I was teaching in the classroom and in the clinical setting on the pediatric unit at the base hospital. I felt it was the best of both worlds. My days were filled with work and preparing for the next day, writing letters to my husband, watching the evening news about the war, going out to eat and shop with friends, and taking piano lessons. I had settled into a routine while counting the days until my husband came home.

In January 1970, Byron arrived back home safely. It was fabulous having him home, and yet my life felt disrupted. For thirteen months, I had eaten out with my friends, cleaned only when I felt like it, spent hours preparing lessons and grading papers, and slept in on Saturday mornings. Fortunately, it didn't take long to get back into married life and spending time with mutual friends.

Several months later, we received thrilling news. I was pregnant. In December 1970, I resigned from my teaching job and delivered a healthy baby boy on January 8, 1971. I became a stay-at-home mom.

When it was time for Byron to reenlist in December 1971, the Vietnam War was still going strong. It was inevitable that he would be sent back for a third tour of duty, so he opted out. The thought of his leaving our son for a year, and possibly forever, was unbearable.

We moved to Wilmington, North Carolina, where he began working in law enforcement. I returned to nursing and began working three evenings a week at the local hospital. My work was satisfying, but I missed teaching.

When the opportunity arose to teach nursing at the University of North Carolina in Wilmington, I jumped on it. We co taught in the classroom. I still remember the day I heard one of my coworkers say while teaching about sexual and physical abuse, "I think what we are seeing and hearing is just the tip of the iceberg." Her words blew my mind. I had never thought of the problem as being rampant but, rather, as occasional aberrancies.

After class, I asked her about her statement. She said, "It's a topic people feel uncomfortable discussing. If we began talking about it more, I think we would hear more and more stories of abuse."

Eventually, we moved to Greensboro, North Carolina, where Byron had taken a job as a polygraph examiner. I began teaching nursing at

Davidson County Community College. For the first time in my teaching career, I was assigned to teach psychiatric nursing and loved it.

After teaching there for four years, it became evident that I would need to get a master of science in nursing (MSN) if I wanted to continue teaching and specialize in one area of nursing. I enrolled in the graduate program at the University of North Carolina in Greensboro in September 1980, to pursue an MSN with a focus on psychiatric nursing education.

FINDING MY NICHE

Group therapy with the teenage girls had been in progress for about twenty minutes. As a graduate student, my role was to be a silent observer. An attractive young female around fourteen or fifteen years old with long brown hair pulled back in a ponytail was speaking. She had been hospitalized two days earlier, after cutting her wrist with a razor blade in a suicide attempt.

"I hate my mom. She came to see me last night and acted all lovey-dovey. That was an act! She's a phony. When I told her that Robbie, her boyfriend, came into my bedroom in the night and raped me, she said I was lying. I begged for her to believe me, but she kept saying I was a liar. The next night, he did it again. I told my mom, and she screamed at me to get out of her house. She grabbed a broom and started swatting me and said she never wanted to see my lying face again. I ran into the bathroom and locked the door, and she began pounding on the door with her fists and yelling at me to get out. I found a razor and cut my wrist. All I wanted to do was die."

Another girl in the group spoke up. "I know what you mean. My mom locks me out of the house when her boyfriend is there. She doesn't care if I'm hungry or cold or whatever. I've had to sleep on the porch all night waiting to get back in. All she cares about is her boyfriend. I swear, if she found me frozen to death on the porch, she'd step over me and keep on walking while complaining that I was in her way. I wish she would die and go to hell." She began sobbing uncontrollably.

I felt a few tears begin to trickle down my cheeks and was hoping no one would notice.

One of the girls pointed at me and said, "Look. She's crying. We made her cry."

Another girl began laughing, and the other girls joined in the laughter. I was perplexed. I wondered what was funny and felt embarrassed and ashamed for crying. Had I done something wrong? It was time for me to learn all I could about physical and sexual abuse.

In 1874, an orphaned nine-year-old, Mary Ellen Wilson, was living with her guardians in New York City's worst tenement. A neighbor heard her screams and wails every day and told a church worker, Etta Wheeler. Etta tried to rescue Mary Ellen by contacting the police, who were unwilling or unable to help. She finally sought help from Henry Bergh, founder of the American Society for the Prevention of Cruelty to Animals (ASPCA).

With the help of his lawyer, they were able to get Mary Ellen removed from her guardians. I was appalled to learn that animals were being protected before children!

Because of Mr. Bergh's interest in protecting children after helping Mary Ellen, a year later the ASPCA created the New York Society for the Prevention of Cruelty to Children (NYSPCC). It was the first child protection agency in the world. Prior to this time, it was acceptable to abuse children. They had very few legal rights, and for the most part, the public condoned child abuse.

Over time, news traveled about what the NYSPCC was doing, and nongovernmental agencies began popping up around the country. In 1899, the world's first juvenile court was established, and in 1912 the federal

Children's Bureau was formed. When the Social Security Act was passed in 1935, it included authorization for the Children's Bureau to work with state agencies to protect neglected children. Even though it included this provision, very little was done due to lack of coordination of services.

In 1946, John Caffey, a pediatric radiologist, published an article describing injuries of young children with subdural hematomas and leg and arm fractures. He hinted at his belief that the injuries were a result of child abuse. Dr. Henry Kempe's interest in child abuse was sparked by Caffey's publication. In 1962, he and his colleagues published an article in the *Journal of the American Medical Association* titled "The Battered Child Syndrome."

Dr. Kempe not only defined child abuse and neglect; he also included many illustrations of types of injuries so that practitioners and others could identify injuries caused by abuse. Included in the paper were instructions on how to report the abuse. He changed the thinking of many by stressing that abuse happened in all socioeconomic classes. Prior to this publication, there was little to no training on the subject for physicians or nurses.

Recognition of sexual abuse lagged behind recognition of physical abuse. In 1897, Sigmund Freud had proposed that the cause of hysteria in the patients he was treating was found in childhood sexual assaults; his colleagues called this preposterous. Ultimately, Freud retracted this theory and proposed a new theory that put responsibility on the victim, who was regarded as fantasizing about having a sexual relationship with her father or paternal figure. Professionals were more comfortable with the belief that sexual assaults were quite rare, and when an assault did occur, it was the consequence of the child's seductive behavior and was not particularly harmful.

Alfred Kinsey, in his 1953 study of female sexual behavior, reported that a quarter of all girls under the age of fourteen reported experiencing some form of sexual assault. There was no public interest in this finding, but the statistics about premarital sex and adultery evoked a huge public outcry.

It wasn't until the early 1970s when the term *sexual abuse* came into use. Prior to that time, it was called a sexual experience, assault, or offense. By 1976, all states had reporting laws requiring professionals to report sexual abuse. In 1977, Dr. Kempe spoke about sexual abuse of children and adolescents and called it another hidden pediatric problem and neglected area.

Prior to my research, I had wondered why physical and sexual abuses were not taught in my classes at the MB Johnson School of Nursing. Learning the history helped me understand that it wasn't until after my graduation that this emerging topic was capturing the interest of health care providers.

Thinking about the way the history of abuse was explained, I thought there was a chance the girls had made up their stories and were laughing because they had pulled something over on me. This explanation didn't feel right. After careful thought, I concluded the girls had not experienced anyone reacting to the gravity of their abuse with heartbreak, and the laughing was their way of attempting to defuse the sadness.

------------- ✚ -------------

In addition to classroom studies, in 1981, I was assigned to do clinical work at a psychiatric hospital. It was a new private hospital for the treatment of adults and adolescents and equipped with a fitness room, movie room, hot tub, and swimming pool. Adult patients were hospitalized for an average of three months and adolescents for nine months to a year. Staff included nurses; mental health associates; social workers; an art, music, movement, and occupational therapist; and a psychologist. The adult unit housed both males and females. All patients were observed at least hourly. If more frequent observations were needed for a patient's safety or the safety of others, he or she could be placed on thirty-minute, fifteen-minute, or one-to-one observation.

The most common diagnoses were major depression, bipolar disorder, schizophrenia, substance abuse, and dementia. Major modes of treatment included group therapy, movement, music and art therapy, socialization skills, and medication management. Psychiatrists from private practices admitted patients and saw them daily. Many of these therapies were new to me, and I loved going to that hospital for my clinical work.

Dr. Ryan, my professor, met with me at the hospital two evenings a week for two weeks. We spent time with patients, chatting and playing board games in the dayroom.

A week later, Dr. Ryan asked me to select a patient for one-on-one time and to record our conversations for analysis.

I chose June. She was an attractive twenty-eight-year old diagnosed with major depression. I mainly listened to what she had to say. She was happily married and had a three-year-old daughter. June's mother had suffered from depression and had committed suicide when June was fourteen years old. June felt responsible for her mother's death. She described herself as a rebellious teenager. Her mother would say, "You're going to be the death of me."

June said, "I'm just like my mother."

"What do you mean by that?"

"I'm depressed. Some days I don't want to get out of bed. I get agitated with my daughter. I tell her to leave me alone, and she walks away crying. I'm not a good mother."

June denied having suicidal thoughts, but I thought she needed closer observation and asked the charge nurse about moving June from hourly to fifteen-minute checks.

She agreed, stating, "I think it's important to listen to our gut feelings."

When I arrived on the unit the following day, June was on one-to-one observation. She had attempted to hang herself in her bedside locker and was found in time.

June avoided eye contact with me and said, "I wanted to die."

"Yes, I know. I'm really glad they found you in time."

"Why?"

"Because I believe you will begin to feel better before long. You're depressed. Depression is an illness just like heart disease and diabetes. The antidepressant you're taking should start working in a few more weeks. It takes about six weeks to eight weeks to begin to feel the antidepressant effect. You've been on Elavil for nearly five weeks."

"I've been depressed all my life. I don't think a pill will work."

"I believe it will. I've seen it work with others, and they felt the same way."

"We'll see."

Her response was hopeful because it sounded like she was willing to wait for the medicine to kick in.

Over the next few weeks, her depression lifted, and she was helping other depressed patients by sharing her story!

While observing group therapy with adult patients, I noted patients were revealing a history of sexual abuse for the first time. It wasn't unusual to hear patients say they had never told anyone about what happened to them. A common theme was that the abuser had told the victim this was their secret. Staff never introduced the topic of sexual abuse, in fear of prompting patients to make up a story.

Listening to their stories was difficult. I wanted to do something, but what? Some of the patients were emotionless as they spoke; others sobbed or expressed extreme anger at their abuser. Many wanted their abuser to acknowledge the abuse. A few made excuses for their abusers, believing it was their fault.

The psychiatrist leading the groups I attended didn't say anything. He let the other patients do the talking. They would ask questions like, "Why didn't you tell your mom?" Or they would simply say, "I'm sorry." A couple of times a group member said, "If that happened to me, I'd kill them."

I realized we still had a long way to go in knowing how to treat the victims and the perpetrators and in debunking the myths.

Adolescents participated in family sessions with a social worker one day a week. I was assigned to attend as an observer. Mom, fifteen-year-old Dana, twelve-year-old Lori, and ten-year-old Debbie were present. They looked like a typical middle-class American family. Mom was dressed in a blue oxford shirt, khaki slacks, and sandals. The girls were wearing colorful T-shirts, shorts, and flip-flops. Dana was in the hospital for depression. Mom's live-in boyfriend was unable to attend because of his work schedule.

Mom was talking about how unruly the girls were, stating, "They don't listen to me. I can't get them to go to bed. They talk back. They don't help around the house. Their rooms are a mess."

The two younger girls were giggling and squirming around in their chairs. Dana sat quietly, watching her sisters.

Miss Johnson, the social worker, asked, "What are the consequences for not listening?"

"I send them to their room, but they just watch TV even when I tell them they are not allowed to."

"What do you do?"

"I don't know what to do."

Lori spoke up, saying, "She yells at us. That's all she ever does."

"And they still don't listen," Mom replied, sounding exasperated.

Miss Johnson said, "So yelling doesn't work. I guess you'll have to try something else."

"That's just it. I don't know what else to do."

"Have you considered taking the TV out of their room?"

"No, but they wouldn't stay in their room if I did that."

The girls giggled.

"What do the girls like to do?"

"Watch TV, hang out with their friends, talk on the phone."

"They sound pretty normal."

"I don't think it's normal. You should be there at bedtime. They stay up half the night watching TV, playing loud music, and running around. I can't get any rest, and my boyfriend tells me I should whip them."

Lori spoke up again, saying, "Sometimes she gives us pot to keep us quiet."

"Is that true?" Miss Johnson asked.

"Yes. It helps them to calm down."

"You know that it's illegal to give them pot."

"I didn't think about that. I just wanted some peace."

"I want you to know that I will have to report this to Child Protective Services. They will have to investigate this."

"Will they take the girls?"

Miss Johnson was silent for a few seconds before responding with "I don't know. They could, but they may refer you for counseling. They'll want to do what is best for you and your children."

The girls had gotten quiet and were listening.

Dana spoke up for the first time saying, "You shouldn't have told her. Now they're are going to take you away from Mom."

Lori said, "You don't care about Mom."

"Yes I do! I just want her to pay more attention to me. She doesn't listen."

Mom looked shocked. "I didn't realize I wasn't listening."

"You always act too busy or bothered when I try to talk to you."

"I'm sorry. I didn't know you thought I didn't care. I love all of you girls, and I don't want to lose you."

Miss Johnson said, "It's about time for our session to end. I'll let the Child Protective Services know that you're working in the family sessions. Maybe she'll consider that when they decide what to do."

"I hope they will."

"Does anyone else have anything to say before we end our session?"

"Can I give my mom a hug?" Dana asked.

"Yes."

Dana got up and walked over to her mom. They gave each other a big hug. When they let go of each other, everyone said goodbye to Dana, and they left the room to go home. Miss Johnson escorted Dana back to the Adolescent Unit.

In 1980, the Adoption Assistance and Child Welfare Act (AACWA) was passed. An emphasis was placed on keeping families together if at all possible. Because of efforts being made to prevent removal of children from their homes, Dana's children were not taken out of their home.

I attended the family session the following week for the last time. For the most part, the girls were more attentive during the session, but they were far from perfect. Mom admitted to having a difficult week, but followed through with her plans. The TV had been removed from the girls' bedroom. Mom said they'd begged, pleaded, and promised to be good if they got the TV back in their room. Mom did not cave in. She said sometimes her nerves were frayed. She reported abstaining from the use of pot to calm herself and the girls. She vowed to keep it out of their home. Her boyfriend was angry about that decision and their relationship was strained. Mom was spending more time paying attention to the girls and paying less attention to him.

Dana was still depressed and in the hospital. The nurses reported she was beginning to participate more in the unit groups and activities.

Plans were made for Mom to start individual therapy. Social Services would be checking in on her and the girls on a regular basis. I hoped the changes would last.

After graduation in 1983, I returned to my job teaching at the local community college. A year later, I resigned and accepted a job at a psychiatric hospital. Surprisingly, my heart was no longer set on teaching but, rather, on practicing psychiatric nursing. It felt right to be back at the bedside.

My first assignment was to work the evening shift on the adult unit. The majority of the patients were admitted for depression, but there were always a handful of patients who were psychotic and others with bipolar disorder (formerly called manic depressive disorder) or schizophrenia. A psychotic person sees, hears, and believes things that others do not experience. Often, their thoughts and what they hear are formidable.

One evening, I admitted a frail seventy-three-year-old female, Mrs. Schnarr. Her matted hair was in a bun, her fingernails were long and dirty, and her dress stained with food. She had been living alone and refusing to allow anyone to enter her home. Her only son brought her meals every day and left them on her front porch. He became more concerned about her when she hadn't picked up the food he had left the previous two days and had called the police. She was admitted to the hospital with an involuntary commitment order.

In North Carolina, anyone who believes an individual is mentally ill and dangerous and needs treatment to prevent further deterioration can go the clerk of court or the magistrate's office and explain why he or she believes the person needs help. If the clerk or magistrate believes the individual meets the criteria for involuntary commitment, a petition for involuntary commitment and a custody order are completed, allowing the sheriff or police to transport the individual to a local mental health facility for evaluation by a psychiatrist. If the physician's examination concurs with the need for involuntary commitment, the clerk or magistrate will issue an order for transportation to an inpatient facility. Within twenty-four hours of admission, a staff physician must examine the patient. If in agreement that the patient needs inpatient care, the physician will hold the patient at the hospital pending a district court hearing.

After making sure I had all the papers leading up to and including the petition for involuntary commitment, I met with Mrs. Schnarr.

"Mrs. Schnarr, my name is Nancy. I'm your nurse this evening. Your son was worried about you. You're here so we can help you feel better."

"My son wants my money. He's been poisoning my food."

"I believe he wants to help you."

She pursed her lips and looked at me menacingly.

"You look scared. What can I do to help?"

She did not answer.

I handed her a hospital gown and asked her to put it on, saying, "I can wash your clothes tonight, and they'll be clean and ready for you in the morning. Also, I need you to pee in this cup. Your doctor wants a urine specimen. You may go in the bathroom to change your clothes and pee in the cup."

I needed her to change into a gown so I could inspect her skin and check her clothes, to be assured she did not have anything in her possession that would be dangerous.

She went into the bathroom and changed into the gown as I watched. I handed her a wipe and instructed her to clean herself before urinating in the cup. Her urine was dark yellow, cloudy, and smelled stronger than normal urine. Her skin was dry, with no bruises or cuts. I removed a safety pin from the hem of her dress. She needed a bath, but I decided to let her rest in bed for a while before suggesting a bath.

"You may get in bed and get some rest," I said, while pulling down the covers. "I'll be back a little later."

She crawled into the bed and pulled the covers up over her.

Later that evening, Dr. Mills arrived. I escorted Mrs. Schnarr to the examination room. After examining her, Dr. Mills found a pair of scissors and told her he needed to cut her hair. The bun on the back of her head was as hard as a rock. We had tried to loosen it up, but it had been so long since her hair had been combed, we could not loosen the hairs. The doctor snipped slowly at the base of the bun until it fell off, hitting the floor with a thud. Mrs. Schnarr jumped and put her hand over her face.

"Are you okay?"

"Someone shot a gun."

"That wasn't a gunshot. That was your hair hitting the floor." I leaned over to pick it up and show it to her.

"That's not my hair."

"Feel the back of your head. Your bun was too matted to comb, so Dr. Mills had to cut it off."

"Where am I?"

"You're in the hospital."

Becoming agitated, she said in a deep growling voice, "I don't need to be in a hospital."

"You have been staying locked up in your home and not eating. Your son was concerned about you. We want to make sure you're okay," Dr. Mills said.

"My son is trying to kill me. There's nothing wrong with me."

"I'm going to do some lab tests to make sure. We'll keep you safe here."

I walked her back to her room and asked her if she wanted to get washed. "A bath will help you feel better."

She agreed to wash at the sink. When finished, she crawled back into her bed. I left her room and reviewed the doctor's orders. He had ordered Haldol.

"Here's some medicine your doctor ordered. It will help you feel calmer and sleep better tonight."

She took the pill from her cup and carefully examined it. After a minute or two, to my surprise, she placed it in her mouth and drank some water. An hour later, she was sleeping soundly.

Mrs. Schnarr stayed in her room the following day. She refused to eat or come out for any activities.

"Hello, Mrs. Schnarr. I'm Nancy, your nurse. Do you remember meeting me yesterday?"

"I don't know you."

"You were tired when you got here. I helped you get ready for bed."

"Where am I?"

"You're at the hospital."

"I want to go home."

"Your doctor is doing some tests. He will let you know when you can go home. Right now, we need to have you stay here. Your son wants to come and see you this evening."

"I don't want to see him!"

"You don't have to see him if you don't want to. If you change your mind, let me know. You can fill out a visitors' list. Visitors will not be permitted unless you put their name on your list. I think your son really wants to see you."

Mrs. Schnarr refused to go to the cafeteria for dinner. I brought her a dinner tray, but she did not eat anything. Later, returning to her room, I sat down to talk with her.

"Are you married?"

"My husband died."

"I'm sorry to hear that. That must be very hard not having him around."

"What do you know? You don't know what it's like."

"You're right. Tell me what it's like."

"My son says I'll get over it. He doesn't know."

"What doesn't he know?"

"I won't get over it!"

"You will never forget your husband. How many years were you married?"

"Forty-eight years."

"That's a long time. You must be very lonely."

She began to sob. I sat quietly with her as she sobbed.

After a while, I told her I was thirsty and wanted to get some milk. I got up, telling her I would be back, and returned with a carton of milk, some graham crackers, and two cups. I opened the carton of milk and poured some in each cup and placed one of the cups and a package of graham crackers in front of her. I opened my pack of graham crackers and began eating them and sipping some milk.

"This tastes good. Those are for you if you would like to have some."

She picked up the cup of milk and drank a little. We continued to talk, and before long, she was eating some graham crackers.

When she finished her milk and crackers, I got up to leave. "I enjoyed my visit with you. We'll have to do this again."

"Yes," she responded.

"Have you thought about allowing your son to visit? I can get the visitors' list, and you can put his name on it."

She agreed to put his name on the list.

Later that evening, her son, Edgar, came to visit.

After their visit, I invited Mrs. Schnarr to come out to the day room and watch TV. She declined. "Maybe tomorrow you'll feel like it."

Arriving the next evening, I found Mrs. Schnarr lying in her bed. The staff reported that she had eaten some prepackaged foods in her room. She still didn't trust the food. The urine culture had come back and showed that Mrs. Schnarr had a urinary tract infection (UTI). Elderly patients may not show the typical signs and symptoms of a UTI. They may become confused, agitated, and paranoid. Dr. Mills ordered an antibiotic.

"Hi, Mrs. Schnarr. It's good to see you. Did you know you have a bladder infection?"

"Yes. My doctor told me."

"The medicine should help you feel better in a few more days."

"That's what he said."

"Was your son able to visit today?"

"No. He said he would come after work."

"Let's surprise him. You can be sitting in the dayroom waiting for him when he comes."

"Where is that?"

"It's not far from your room. Would you like to see it?"

She sat up and put on her shoes. We walked to the dayroom.

"This is nice. Am I allowed to watch TV?"

"Yes. Would you like a snack?"

"What do you have?"

"Come with me to the kitchen. You can see your choices and pick out what you want."

She walked with me to the galley, and after carefully scrutinizing what was available, she chose some vanilla pudding. We returned to the dayroom, where she sat at a small table and opened the pudding.

Kathy, a mental health tech, was doing fifteen-minute checks. I called her over and introduced her to Mrs. Schnarr. "Kathy will come around frequently. If you need anything, let her know. She can take you to the cafeteria for dinner. You will have more choices of what you want to eat. I'm going to go do some other things. Enjoy your pudding."

Mrs. Schnarr did not say anything. At least she didn't balk at the idea. When it was time for dinner, Mrs. Schnarr got up and walked with the other patients to the cafeteria. I smiled to myself and thought, *I believe the Haldol is working. She isn't as paranoid or frightened.* I figured that, in a few more days, the antibiotic should be working and would help her mind clear even more.

Over the next two weeks, Mrs. Schnarr continued to improve. She began attending group therapy, the grief/loss group, and the movement therapy group. Staff reported that she had begun to participate in the groups. Nearly every evening upon my arrival, Mrs. Schnarr was sitting in the dayroom. Her grooming had improved, and her son reported she was getting back to her normal self.

Dr. Mills planned to keep her on the Haldol until a few days before her discharge. She was tolerating it well and wasn't showing any signs of paranoia. If her symptoms returned, he planned to order a small daily dose. She would most likely be discharged in another week or two.

A newly admitted young male who was totally naked walked into the dayroom where other patients were sitting and began yelling, "I'm Jesus Christ. Humble yourself before me, or I'll humble you."

A couple staff members rushed to the area. Bill, a mental health tech, choosing not to address the young man as Jesus Christ said, "Brandon, come with—"

Before he could finish his sentence, Brandon lunged toward the tech yelling, "I'm Jesus Christ!" and began throwing punches at Bill.

Bill ducked and stepped back.

Sierra, one of the nurses, ran into the nursing station and paged three times, "Code One, Adult Unit Dayroom."

Within seconds, it sounded like a stampede coming down the hall and barreling through the double doors. All available staff had rushed to the unit. When they saw Bill ducking as the patient threw punches, they rushed toward Brandon and wrestled him to the floor. At least seven staff huddled over him, struggling to hold him down. He began yelling obscenities as he fought to free himself.

This was my first observation of a Code One. I was frightened and felt pity for the patient, fearing he or one of the staff would get hurt.

Ann, a mental health tech, asked the nurse, "Do I need to set up a seclusion room?"

"Yes."

The seclusion room, located off the unit, had high ceilings, cinder block walls, and a concrete floor. In the middle of the room, a heavy metal bed sat bolted to the floor. It was made from one piece of metal, had no sharp edges, and had slots all along the sides and ends of the platform that held the mattress. Restraint straps could be threaded through the slots, fastened, and locked in place. A large metal door with a small window was the only entrance into the room.

Ann scurried off to set up the room, gathering locking wrist, ankle, and waist restraints along the way. Using the key she'd received during orientation, she locked them to the bed.

The staff rolled Brandon on his abdomen, lifted him, and carried him facedown to the seclusion room. He fought the entire time, causing staff to stumble over each other along the way. It was a pitiful sight. They placed him on his back on the bed. Bill applied the restraints as staff struggled to keep Brandon from wiggling loose. Brandon continued to holler and threatened to sue Bill.

Sierra spoke softly to Brandon, saying, "We don't want to hurt you. When you are calmer and not threatening to hurt the staff or other patients, you can go back to your room."

I didn't think he heard a word she said because he was yelling the whole time she was speaking.

The staff exited the room and locked the door. Sierra called Brandon's doctor. He ordered a Haldol 5 mg injection stat. The doctor would have to come to the hospital and see the patient within an hour. Sierra prepared and gave the injection as staff helped hold him still. He screamed and squirmed as best he could.

Haldol was one of ten or more antipsychotic drugs available since the first one, chlorpromazine (Thorazine), was introduced in the mid-1950s for the treatment of schizophrenia and was called a major tranquilizer. The classification of it was changed to neuroleptic and, later, an antipsychotic. Today, there are newer antipsychotic drugs available, but Haldol continues to be used, since it's just as effective as the newer ones and costs significantly less.

Dr. Scott arrived within an hour. Brandon was still agitated and threatening the staff. Dr. Scott ordered an additional 5 mg Haldol injection and Haldol 5 mg every four hours as needed for agitation.

While Brandon was in seclusion, the mental health tech checked him every fifteen minutes and offered fluids. Every hour, the nurse checked his vital signs and released his restraints, one at a time, to exercise his arms and legs. Brandon fell asleep after receiving the second injection of Haldol. He was released back to his room an hour later and slept through the night.

Later that evening, during visiting hours, I met Brandon's parents. His mom recounted the events leading up to Brandon's admission, saying, "Brandon graduated from college a year and a half ago with a bachelor of arts in psychology and moved back home. He was unable to find employment, gave up looking after several months, and withdrew to his room to read his Bible for hours at a time.

"The morning of his admission, I suggested he fill out some job applications. He began pacing and was obviously upset, saying his college professors were keeping him from getting a job. When I asked him why they would try to keep him from finding work, he said they were afraid of his power because they knew who he really was.

"I suggested that he see a psychiatrist. That really ticked him off. He accused me of being the devil and ordered me to get out of his room.

"Frightened and shaking, I called Don, my husband. He rushed home and sprinted upstairs to talk with our son. Brandon had the door to his room barricaded with the dresser and bed and refused to let his dad come in. Don called the police. After several hours, they were able to persuade him to come out of his room, and subsequently, he was admitted to the hospital."

His mother was crying as she gave his history. Don sat quietly as she talked. When she finished, he said, "He was a good boy. I can't believe this is happening. Right after Brandon graduated, he told me something happened when he was away at college. I asked him about it, but he did not want to tell me. When he didn't get a job, I thought he was lazy. We got into a lot of arguments about him not getting a job, but nothing changed. Over time, I realized Brandon was no longer the same boy we'd had before he went to college. I wanted my son back but didn't know what to do."

Don's eyes filled with tears. Hearing their story broke my heart.

Brandon's doctor diagnosed him with paranoid schizophrenia. Brandon and his parents attended therapy sessions with their assigned social worker. They were given information about his illness and how it could be managed, and it was suggested they attend support groups offered by the National Alliance on Mental Illness (NAMI) for families and friends dealing with mental illness.

Brandon attended group therapy and art and music therapy during the day. In the evenings, he came to a relaxation group. He was calmer on his medication, although he continued to believe he had special powers from God. After several months of inpatient treatment, he was discharged home with his family.

About a year later, the hospital offered a training program on managing aggressive behavior. We learned how to block punches and kicks; how to escape from headlocks, chokes, bites, and having our hair pulled; and how to safely take down a patient. For two days, a group of twelve participants practiced the techniques, and on the third day, each member was tested individually by the instructors. Participants of the program who scored 100 on the test became instructors. They taught the program to all clinical staff. The number of injuries decreased as a result of the training and the staff working together as a team.

I had been working at the hospital ten years when I was transferred to an outpatient program. Patients who did not need inpatient care but required more intense care than a counselor or physician's office could provide came during the day and returned home in the evening. They attended various groups throughout the day, and their psychiatrist saw them at least one time a week.

Mr. Patrick Williams, a thin, sad-looking, though neatly groomed middle-aged male, was admitted to our program by Dr. Jones. Patrick had worked as a machine operator in a textile factory for many years, but for the past year had been on disability due to severe depression. His diagnosis was treatment-resistant major depressive disorder, and he was chronically suicidal. He and his wife had two adult married daughters and three grandchildren.

Dr. Jones had tried treating him with many different antidepressants and electroconvulsive therapy. He was currently taking one of the monoamine oxidase inhibitors (MAOIs), Parnate. This type of antidepressant was normally used as a last resort because of the dietary restrictions necessary to prevent a hypertensive crisis. Foods that contain high amounts of tyrosine, a naturally occurring protein that creates tyramine when it is broken down in the body, must be avoided. Examples of foods containing tyrosine include bananas, raspberries, overripe fruits, chocolate, caffeinated beverages, draft beer, red wine, hot dogs, pepperoni, salami, bologna, yogurt, and aged cheeses. The Parnate was ineffective, just as the other meds had been.

A new class of antidepressants had hit the US market. They were known as SSRIs (selective serotonin reuptake inhibitors). SSRIs targeted serotonin, a specific neurotransmitter that was believed to be deficient in the brain of persons with depression. This new class of antidepressants helped increase the amount of serotonin available. Dr. Jones tapered the dose of Parnate, and after it was stopped completely, he waited two weeks before starting Mr. Williams on Prozac. It was the first SSRI introduced in our country. It would take four to six weeks to know whether it would work.

It didn't. He tried several other new drugs on the market, but none of them helped.

Mr. Williams attended the outpatient program for a little over a year. Every day he was the same—no change in his depression or suicidal thoughts. Dr. Jones decided to discharge him from the program. He would see him weekly in his office. I was concerned that Mr. Williams would attempt suicide, but Mr. Williams was okay with the plan to quit the program and to be followed by his doctor. Occasionally, I asked Dr. Jones about Mr. Williams. The report was always the same—no change in his depression.

One afternoon as I was leaving the hospital, I met Mr. Williams coming through the front door.

"Hi Nancy," he said.

"Mr. Williams! How are you?"

"I'm doing great," he said with a smile on his face and looking ten years younger. "One morning, I woke up, and the depression was gone. It was like I had leaped out of a black hole. That was about two months ago. At first I was afraid of falling back in it, but I'm beginning to feel more hopeful. Thanks for never giving up on me. You, Dr. Jones, and all the others kept cheering me on. I owe my life to all of you. I probably would have killed myself without the help I received."

"What an amazing story. I'm so happy for you."

"I came to see my daughter. She's depressed like I was. I come to see her every day to cheer her on and to remind her that she will get through it just like I did."

"You're a living testimony. She's fortunate to have you there for her."

We talked for a few more minutes before he went inside to see his daughter. Joyously, I walked to my car.

Jamie, a woman in her midthirties, was admitted with a diagnosis of borderline personality disorder. I had never heard of this disorder until I began working at the hospital. Quickly, I found it was challenging working with patients with this disorder. It is characterized by extreme mood swings, troubled relationships, highly impulsive behaviors, and destructive behaviors such as drug and alcohol abuse, burning or cutting oneself, and suicide attempts. Jamie struggled with feelings of abandonment and feeling empty. Her mother had died of a drug overdose several years previously. Repeatedly, she talked about how much she missed her mother, idealizing her as a perfect mother, even though her descriptions revealed Jamie had been neglected as a child. She was suspicious of others and described sitting in her yard at night smoking marijuana and watching her neighbors. At times, she expressed suicidal thoughts. Jamie had a husband and two children. She never talked about them.

One morning, Jamie arrived extremely agitated and remained agitated throughout the morning. She abruptly walked out of the group at one point but returned several minutes later.

Around noon, the group broke up for a lunch break. One of the co leaders from another group, Sonya, approached me and asked what that bulge was at the top of Jamie's shirt. I hadn't noticed the bulge and asked my co leader to take our patients to the cafeteria while Sonya asked Jamie to stay behind to talk with us.

After everyone was gone, Sonya asked Jamie, "What do you have in your shirt?"

Jamie pulled out a small handgun and pointed it at Sonya.

My heart was racing, but somehow I managed to say, "Jamie, I don't want you to hurt anyone. We want to help you."

She turned, aimed the gun at me, and said, "Take it from me."

Fortunately, I remembered the importance of remaining calm and to never try to take a gun from someone. A struggle might ensue and someone could get shot. So, in my calmest voice, I said, "I want you to lay the gun on the table."

"Go ahead. Take it from me."

Sonya spoke up, saying, "We want you to lay it on the table."

She continued to talk to Jamie. I slipped away to lock the door leading into our area. I contemplated paging Code W in outpatient to alert hospital staff that someone had a weapon and to stay out of the area. If that code were paged, the police were to be notified. I was afraid that, if I paged the code, Jamie might get more agitated and shoot me or even both of us. Instead, I walked back over to Sonya and Jamie. She and Sonya continued talking. All the while Jamie kept the gun aimed. I was amazed at how calm Sonya sounded. After what seemed like an eternity but was actually ten to fifteen minutes, Jamie laid the gun on the table.

"Jamie, come with me. I'm going to take you to the Adult Unit and call your doctor," I said.

It was against hospital policy to take a person to the unit until they were admitted. I decided to go against the policy. Jamie calmly walked with me. Once on the unit, I asked her to have a seat in the dayroom while I called her doctor. I left her and entered the nursing station. I told the staff what was going on and called Dr. Phillips. He instructed us to strip-search Jamie and take her to a seclusion room. He would be right over. The staff took over Jamie's care, and I left to find Sonya.

I found her outside sitting on the ground holding the gun. There were bullets lying on the ground beside her. She told me the gun had been loaded and the safety was off. Fortunately, she was familiar with guns and knew how to unload it safely. When Dr. Phillips arrived, he made arrangements to transfer Jamie to the state hospital.

I didn't see Jamie for nearly two years. One day, I was in line at the grocery store when I heard someone yell my name and say in a threatening tone, "You made me go to the hospital."

Startled, I looked up and saw Jamie in the same checkout lane with three customers separating us. In a calm voice I said, "Jamie, wait until you get through the line, and I'll talk with you."

I had no intention of talking to her. As soon as my groceries were checked out, I scurried to my car, heaved the bags in the trunk, and sped off. That was the last time I saw Jamie.

I continued working at the psychiatric hospital until retiring in 2009. My decision to retire wasn't easy. I loved nursing; however, the changes taking place didn't feel right to me. It seemed like the insurance companies were dictating patient care. They were the determiners of the length of stay. The time was shortened to three days for adult patients and seven days for children and adolescents, making the inpatient population more acute. It seemed that nurses' opinions did not matter. I was not opposed to short stays if the patient was ready for discharge. Hospital administrators had to look at the bottom line and were pressured to cut costs; as a result, staffing numbers decreased. I knew it was time for me to leave, and so with some ambivalence, I turned in my letter of resignation.

EPILOGUE

During my last few months of employment, I found myself telling stories to my coworkers, friends, and family about my early years in nursing. I loved sharing what was expected of nurses and how we were to dress and care for our patients. Only then, as I reminisced, did it dawn on me the explosion of knowledge that had taken place through the years. The changes happened at a slow, steady pace, barely noticeable. Yet the accumulated magnitude made a huge impact on the delivery of nursing care.

The younger nurses were shocked to learn about the equipment we reused. Gone are those days. No more sharpening needles and sterilizing glass syringes. No more glass IV bottles, metal bedpans, and mercury thermometers.

I never imagined that what was then considered state of the art would become obsolete. With the explosion of technology, physicians have equipment that makes earlier diagnoses possible with greater accuracy. Nurses now use digital equipment to monitor blood pressure and pulse rate and glucometers to check blood sugar levels. Other new tools include IV infusion pumps, heart monitors, defibrillators, and ventilators. Computers are used to measure the pressure inside a patient's heart and the amount of oxygen in the blood. The death rate from heart disease has decreased. Cancer survival rates are up 30 percent since the 1960s.

It was once normal for new mothers and their babies to remain in the hospital for ten days. Following cataract, gallbladder, and hernia surgery, patients were usually hospitalized two weeks. Improved technology has decreased hospital stays and, in some cases, the need to be hospitalized for a procedure.

Large incisions are no longer needed. Instruments with cameras can be inserted through tiny incisions. The surgeon watches his movements on a screen while using small instruments to repair a hernia or remove a gallbladder. Patients are back home in twenty-four hours or less.

Cataracts are removed by using ultrasound to break the opaque lens into tiny pieces. The pieces are suctioned out through a miniscule incision. Following this short procedure, patients return home within half an hour.

Many nurses now specialize in a specific area, allowing them to become experts in that field. They are able to keep up with the latest technology, medicine, and research in their chosen area. It would be nearly impossible to keep up with the changes across the entire field of health care.

Vaccines have nearly eradicated rubella and mumps. I recall hearing in nursing school that we knew every disease that existed. Obviously, that was misinformation. Since graduating, I have learned about HIV infections, AIDS, SARS, Legionnaires' disease, West Nile virus, Lyme disease, Reye's syndrome, and the Zika virus. I wonder how many more will be discovered.

The number of medications available has more than doubled. There are automated computerized drug storage devices that electronically dispense medications. Using a password to access the system, nurses find the patient's name and a list of medications ordered for that patient and select the medication needed. Then a drawer opens and delivers the medication requested. The device tracks the person who accessed the system, the patient's name, and the medication removed. It is believed that using this system decreases errors and nurses have quicker access to newly ordered medications.

It is hard to imagine that many of these new technological devices could become antiquated fifty years from now. Who knows what the future holds?

Over fifty-five years ago, I chose to become a nurse because I wanted to make a difference in people's lives just like our family doctor and my sister Joyce. It has been an awesome journey, bringing more joy than I could have imagined.

We sang Dorothy Alexander's "My Creed" often at MB Johnson School of Nursing. The closing lyrics of this song sum up my journey as a nurse:

> And when with tired feet I come,
> For rough are roads that must be trod;
> Then may He say, "Thy work's well done,"
> You have walked hand in hand with God.

87786279R00128

Made in the USA
Middletown, DE
05 September 2018